DATE DUE

FAMILY-CENTERED PRACTICE

The Interactional Dance beyond the Family System

FAMILY-CENTERED PRACTICE

The Interactional Dance beyond the Family System

John Victor Compher, M.S.S.

Foreword by
Edgar H. Auerswald, M.D.

HUMAN SCIENCES PRESS, INC.

Library of Congress Cataloging in Publication Data

Compher, John Victor.
    Family-centered practice: the interactional dance beyond the family system / by
John Victor Compher.
    p.   cm.
    Bibliography: p.
    ISBN 0-89885-422-9
    1. Problem families — Counseling of — United States. 2. Family social work — United
States. 3. Social work with the socially handicapped — United States. 4. Social work
with children — United States. I. Title.
HV699.C545   1989   87-36143
362.8′28′0973 — dc19   CIP

Parts of Chapters 2, 4, 6, 12, and 14 are adapted from the following published articles
of the author, and are reprinted with the kind permission of the journals in which the
articles appeared:

"The Dance Beyond the Family System," copyright 1987, National Association of
Social Workers, Inc. Reprinted with the permission of *Social Work,* March–April 1987,
Vol. 32, No. 2, pp. 105–108.

"The Case Conference Revisited: A Systems View," *Child Welfare,* September 1984,
pp. 411–418.

"Home Services to Families to Prevent Child Placement," copyright 1983. Reprinted
with the permission of *Social Work,* September–October 1983, pp. 360–364.

"Parent–School–Child Systems: Triadic Assessment and Intervention," *Social Casework,*
September 1982, pp. 415–423.

© 1989 John Victor Compher
Human Sciences Press, Inc., is a subsidiary of
Plenum Publishing Corporation
233 Spring Street, New York, N.Y. 10013

Printed in the United States of America

To Elaine B. Jackson
An inspired teacher and practitioner
of human service

FOREWORD

Something exciting is happening in our twentieth century. Like a butterfly in metamorphosis, our human species is emerging not only from the confines of our planet, but also from the cocoon of past awareness. A new version of what we call reality is forming at an accelerating rate. We are as a result redefining our history and recasting our destiny.

This creative transformation in our definition and understanding of reality showed up first at the turn of the century in the events that gave birth to relativity and quantum physics. It has resulted in the emergence of some totally new domains of scientific endeavor. One of these is the science of ecology, which is the study of patterns of events in the natural environment of our planet. Another is chaos theory, which posits that order emerges from randomness. A third is systems theory, which developed a language and techniques for studying the similarities and differences found in the dynamics of various commonly occurring event patterns. Still another is cybernetics, in which linear causation has been replaced by a model in which causation and stability in a system are thought of as the outcome of interrelated recursive patterns that control each other. All of these new domains of science have changed the meaning of coincidence. In fact, the word "coincidence" is no longer in use in those domains. While those naturally occurring patterns of events that were formerly discarded as the outcome of pure coincidence are no longer seen as one-time random occurrences. In the larger context provided by the new science, they appear as recurrent patterns in which form may be observed.

Some fifty or more years after this transformation began to take root in physics, the assumptions and the way of thinking that emerged there reached the domain that spawned this book—the behavioral sciences. It first showed up in the birth of what is now known as the family therapy movement.

The founders of this movement consisted of a small group of psychotherapists, mostly psychiatrists or psychologists, who had become tired of approaching their tasks reductionistically. They were rebelling against a diagnostic system that required them to consider all aberrant psychological states to be pathological, and to search for the sources of such pathology only inside the individuals who exhibited them. Many had noted the failure of behavioral and biological science to develop a clear and consistent consensual understanding of the grab bag of aberrant states that they had been taught to label schizophrenia. They hypothesized that the phenomenon of schizophrenia might be the outcome of recurrent interactional patterns in the families of those so diagnosed.

These rebellious behavioral scientists thus changed their basic assumptions and their way of thinking in precisely the same way as had the physicists. They abandoned their former reductionistic, atomistic, mechanistic way of thinking and turned to the study of connected patterns of events in the lives of their clients.

Because of the rigorous empiricism of physics—the requirement that new discoveries must be amenable to mathematical expression—new assumptions that replace old assumptions attain stability until they too are eventually replaced. Not so in the behavioral sciences, where such rigor is difficult to attain. Thus, although family therapy has grown rapidly into a separate and recognized discipline, much of what has occurred in that process, has too often been based on the old assumptions. The epistemological transformation that generated and characterized the beginnings of the movement has stayed alive, however, and the numbers of those who have made the shift have increased. The body of work based on the new assumptions has continued to grow.

Recognizing that their way of thought was congruent with
the thought of the new sciences of ecology and systems theory,
that segment of the field whose work is based on the new assumptions has borrowed the terms. They now refer to themselves as ecosystemic family therapists. Not surprisingly, the data
with which this group work, in both therapy and research, consist of descriptions of patterns of events in the fields of their
clients' lives that contain and explain the distress that brought
their clients to them. They describe these events in narrative
form. They tell stories and, together with the families they work
with, invent interventions designed to create endings for these
stories in which the desired therapeutic results are achieved.

This brings us to the events that have resulted in this book.
As early as 1965 a few ecosystemic therapists began to realize,
that to complete the stories they sought, they frequently had to
widen the domain of their search to a field larger than the family. They had to include elements from the physical, cultural,
and socioeconomic surroundings in which families live. That
this discovery was made by ecosystemic therapists who had decided to work with economically poor families is not surprising.
The distress of poor people always includes elements that originate in the socioeconomic domain.

A concomitant discovery made by these therapists was that,
if they limited their work to activities carried out in the confin-
ing space of an office, their vantage point was unduly restricted.
Those elements of the story that were located outside the family system were often not visible. Even if they could hypothesize
those elements by piecing together information brought to them,
they could not verify their hypotheses while sitting in an office.
Also, some of the interventions required to bring the story to
its desired ending could not be carried out there. They came to
the conclusion that they would have to become mobile; they
would have to acquire the freedom to move about in the communities in which their clients lived.

Given the freedom to move around a poor community looking at it in an ecosystemic frame, one sees a massively fragmented system of services. It is a terrain occupied by a plethora
of hierarchically organized, categorized service organizations,
each of which has defined its mission as a response to *part* of
the lives of the people it serves. These organizations have not

been formed simultaneously within a plan in which each is assigned a segment of a complete spectrum of services and in which procedures for efficient articulation between each of the cogs in such a machine have been clearly spelled out. Instead, each has its own history and internally generated commitments and, in the interest of survival, each promotes its own vested interests and protects its boundaries. Agency functions overlap, and no community has agencies that form a comprehensive whole. There are parts missing, and some categories of distress go unattended.

To carry out its mission, each organization has engaged in self-definition, and has developed its own language and its own book of rules that have grown with a central focus on the piece of life the organization has decided to address. These organizations seldom talk to each other; when they do, they can only communicate in those areas in which the language they use denotes common meaning. Each operates with a reductionistic thought style, and each has developed a reductionistic procedural sequence that functions to identify and discard events that seem random or coincidental. The field in which events are considered relevant shrinks progressively as these procedures are followed, and the fullness of identity and capacities and strengths of those served become obscured in a process that only defines their problems.

Distressed people who seek services, or helpers who are assisting them, have to decide in what category their distress belongs; they must then roam around on this fragmented terrain, seeking out the organization that delivers help for *that* category. Complex situations have to be broken down into parts, so that each part fits the definition of some agency, and a number of agencies must then be found.

If one observes this terrain ecosystemically for any sustained time, one cannot avoid coming to the conclusion that, taken as a whole, the system currently providing services, especially that providing services to those who live in the ghettos populated by America's poor, not only is ineffective and inefficient in its response to individuals and families whose distress has complex roots, but also can *create problems* for those it purports to serve. It can, in fact, be downright toxic. Furthermore, it is often blind to its own iatrogenic toxicity.

The most astonishing observation of all, however, is that this system has been designed and developed, and is currently manned, by intelligent, usually compassionate, concerned people who are all thinking rationally. They are all making common sense in the traditional Western thought mode, each in his or her particular role in a particular fragment of the system. Just as the methods of formal research that have emerged from the mechanistic, atomistic, reductionistic thought/reality system of the industrialized world cannot study these complex iatrogenic phenomena, the service system that has emerged from the same thought/reality system cannot respond to such phenomena.

Ecosystemic thinkers who observe this reality cannot help but be seized with a sense of urgency. They are in a strange position. They cannot confront the problem head on. They cannot cure the blind spot of a society that is blind to the existence of its blind spot. There are a couple of actions they can engage in, however. One is to teach others to think ecosystemically. The other is to become storytellers and bring the ecosystemic stories they encounter that expose iatrogenesis to as wide an audience as possible. One way to do that is to publish them.

That is the point of this book. Its author sits at the growing edge of the twentieth-century scientific endeavor. He is an ecosystemic thinker who has been working in the human service system in a community, and he understands the importance of his experience. He is publishing his stories, replete with his own ideas as to what can be done to hasten the needed transformation. He has also invented language that can be added to the glossary of research and practice in ecosystemic reality, and tested for its usefulness.

This is why I think I am accurate when I describe this as a book in which the author first presents scientific data in the form of stories that describe his work as a therapist in front-line community services; second, does an ecosystemic critique of those stories in such a way as to expose systemic dysfunctions that can damage clients; and third, illustrates opportunities and methods for resolving many of these difficulties in practice.

It is one of the few such books around; others who work as therapists or helping professionals, within and without community-based services, and those interested in improving such

services will learn from it. The book is a significant effort that
I hope will inspire others to follow the author's lead.

Edgar H. Auerswald, M.D.

ACKNOWLEDGMENTS

During the writing of this book a number of individuals have kindly read various sections and offered encouragement and helpful suggestions. I am especially appreciative in this regard to Happy Fernandez of Temple University School of Social Administration and to the late Eudice Glassberg, also of this school.

Many other persons, including former supervisors or teachers, such as Muriel Shapp of The Philadelphia Child Guidance Clinic, Carolyn Needleman of Bryn Mawr College School of Social Work and Social Research, and Samuel Kirschner of The Institute of Comprehensive Family Therapy, along with particular colleagues, friends, and my wife, Charlene, have all added richly to my professional and personal development, thereby in both direct and indirect ways contributing to the experiential and intellectual foundations which undergird the family-centered practice I describe in this book. To all of these special people, those named and unnamed, I am most grateful.

CONTENTS

INTRODUCTION

The dance or interactional relationships of the professionals and the families with whom they operate, either simultaneously or sequentially, is an emerging new area in the family systems field that requires exploration. My own participation in this larger system, first as a family therapist in a private suburban agency setting, then as a family-oriented social worker in a public welfare program for truant or delinquent youth and, more recently, as a child protective services supervisor and trainer in an urban family-based organization, has provided a number of vantage points.

Through exploration, for example, in recent years of the family's essentially triadic relationship with the school system, I became aware that the interactive style of the school personnel, parents, and child is a key factor in determining the quality of the child's educational experience. Similarly, the quality and manner of the relationship of families to other professionals in the concrete social service context, as well as the various helpers' own relationships to each other, determine how effectively treatment and service goals can be achieved.

With clients who are not always voluntary participants in the larger social service or educational systems, I have observed this dance to be all the more significant and graphic. In the contexts of child welfare, delinquency services, or the public schools, there is often no single social agent willing or able to take charge of cohesive treatment or service planning; and it is not uncommon for the client (or student) to become lost in a maze of seemingly random, incoherent, or conflictual forces. This very negative process may interplay with the client's personal or familial dysfunctions in such ways as to keep the client disengaged and yet dependent upon the chaotic service system—at times, over several family generations.

In addition to this lateral terrain of the family, i.e., its social interfaces, a second significant area of interest for me has been the systemic depth of the family or its vertical territory. Beyond the immediate interactional system of the family which has indeed been the focus of the family therapy movement since its inception, there are clearly also deeper-level functions that emerge from powerful systemic introjects or isomorphs within the family's history. These processes come into play, recognized or not, with any comprehensive treatment service to families, whether through the orchestration of positive transferential experiences in a clinical setting or the development of intimate professional ties between a client family and team of social workers in an impoverished public housing project. Unfortunately, both the psychodynamic and systems schools, through almost exclusive interest in the diagnosis and treatment of either individuals or families per se, have failed to fully recognize and to integrate these lateral and vertical dimensions of the family.

This book seeks to address these often-overlooked horizontal and deeper regions beyond or within the family system and to suggest interventions which lead to more cohesive and significant levels of treatment and service planning. My approach, however, is not a purely theoretical one, since in addition to the expository chapters I have also written a number of dramatic vignettes about the families being serviced. The vignettes, fully disguised to protect confidentiality, are drawn largely from child welfare and educational contexts and will, it is hoped, provide the reader a more vivid sense of the internal and external struggles of the distressed family as it battles within itself and at the same time reacts to the often chaotic social systems around it. Both poignant and upbeat, the stories are intentionally selected to illustrate how the application of sufficient contextual and clinical skills and carefully organized services can indeed

produce positive outcomes in many instances, even against the
seemingly overwhelming odds within a client's social context.
Unlike traditional academic case studies, these vignettes,
which alternate between the theoretical chapters, seek to de-
pict, through dramatic dialogue, first-person narration of the
social worker or client, descriptive passages or other literary
conventions, the flesh and blood of the experience of working
in the large service context with very troubled and, in most of
these instances, involuntary client families. In the opening case
story, "Future," for instance, the children, relatives, and friends
of a mother who was a former intravenous drug abuser and
who died of AIDS, struggle to survive together and to find
meaning in a community context which was initially quite hostile and rejecting. In "Losing His Turn," a child of a ruptured
working-class family walks the thin ice between institutional
placement and remaining with his ambivalent father in the community. In "Madonna of the Park," a five-year-old boy who has
almost miraculously survived child sexual abuse and a mysteri-
ous fall from the 13th floor of his housing project building, experiences the frustration and joy of a visit with his beautiful but
incompetent mother. In all of these vignettes, the human experience is highlighted while the delivery of services provides
a backdrop.

The alternating chapters discuss, among other things, a
number of typical service system dances within several contexts,
the theoretical underpinnings of the comprehensive treatment
process, the cross-cultural dimension of services for minority
clients, and the impact of the bureaucratic agency upon service
delivery. In contrast to the vignettes, these expository chapters
often illustrate or emphasize the more dysfunctional and negative interactional processes of the various participants of the
system. For purposes of discussion, various rubrics are created
and assigned to these patterns which suggest the characteristic
dynamic of the behaviors or interactional dances.

More specifically, Chapter 2 describes some quite common
problematic system dances or behavioral configurations of the
multiservice professionals who interact simultaneously with the
client. This chapter also outlines viable means for reorganizing
the client's immediate service system.

The family's interface with the school system, potentially the most influential of the extrafamilial systems impacting the family, is the subject of Chapter 4. Several basic triadic interactional assessment modes are outlined; while in Chapter 6 methods of intervention and examples of dealing effectively with the family–school–child interface are provided.

Chapter 8 discusses the cross-cultural dance between the social worker and the client of different ethnic backgrounds. And Chapter 10 provides a clinical foundation for these team approaches which bridges family systems theory, psychodynamic, and object relations thinking. The sum of these theoretical parts creates a greater whole—e.g., the emergent concept of powerful early triadic systemic introjects which may be influenced through systemic team treatment. This approach, described under the rubric "systonic teams," is a personalized and adaptive team process in which both professionals and, at times, laypersons from the client's informal network contract to work jointly with the client family on specific personal transactional, intrapsychic, or problematic social or community issues.

Chapter 12 revisits the time-honored case management process and case conference, discussing these modes from a wholistic or systems perspective. Chapter 14 outlines an optimal continuum of family-based services, simpler modes advancing to complex interagency team modalities, depending upon the specific client family's relative level of concrete and therapeutic needs.

Finally, Chapter 16 illustrates how the large bureaucratic service agency, seeming typically to exist unto itself, profoundly affects the family system. A laundry list of the "dirty dozen" dysfunctional dynamics, which negatively influence service outcomes, is described, with recommendations for significant higher-level systems changes.

Chapter 1

FUTURE
A Vignette

The vignette "Future" describes an impoverished young, black, single-parent family whose mother, a former intravenous drug abuser, is dying of acquired immune deficiency syndrome (AIDS). The breakdown of this family is exacerbated by the initial rejections of the health care system and the original hysteria of the social service organizations who were mandated to provide services. Family-oriented services eventually intervene successfully, however, (1) to assist the family to acknowledge and to express their grief, (2) to support officially the mother's arrangements to keep all of the children together with a young caretaker couple within the family's church and friendship system, and (3) to facilitate responsible communication through case conferencing among a disorganized and divided service community. The family is also discussed briefly in Chapter 2, under the section, "The Rejecting System."

Although the air-conditioning in the hospital was on, my hands sweated profusely under the rubber surgical gloves. The white mask was restrictive, while the oversized paper gown I had also been given to wear refused to close properly and flapped around my arms. Perhaps the dying patient would laugh when she met me and that would break the ice. It would be an unusual initial meeting with a client. Many questions ran through my mind as I waited outside her door. Could rapport and trust be built through our conversation and eye contact? How many

1

other medical personnel and social workers had Ms. Morrisey already met today? What would she want to know about her children?

Ms. Morrisey had been diagnosed a number of months ago as an AIDS (acquired immune deficiency syndrome) patient. She had contracted the disease through a former intravenous drug habit. Now she lived in an isolated, sterile environment —at least when she was in the hospital. Aside from her 14-year-old daughter, Lydia, and Mr. Whitaker, who presently helped her to take care of the younger children, there were no visitors. Everyone but the medical personnel seemed too afraid to be near her and the young children were not permitted to go to her room. Only the characters of the ever-present TV soap operas seemed undaunted and willing to spend long hours with her. Occasionally she imagined that God or his counterparts were there and speaking to her. Perhaps they had found a way to sneak into the room without wearing the full medical regalia.

Prior to this second hospitalization, Ms. Morrisey and her family had been through a very considerable ordeal. Too weak to care for herself and her four children (besides Lydia, there were three sons, aged eleven, nine, and two), she and the children had all moved into her sister's small apartment. The sister knew little about the disease or its potential hazards. When the general hysteria over AIDS hit the newspapers and the nation, a nurse told her that the mother should stay in a separate room, eat off her own dinnerware, use her own private toilet, and that clothing and bed linens should be washed separately. Such precautions were impossible in the aunt's very crowded apartment. And besides, Ms. Morrisey, though quite weak, was also annoyed at such notions and would not cooperate with these difficult precautions.

Within this stressful setting, old conflicts had also erupted between the sisters, creating an acrimonious environment for the children as well. Everyone felt trapped, and the home had become a pressure cooker of angry, frightened people, resulting in reports from neighbors of alleged physical abuse against two of the children.

Since line workers from the agency were intimidated by

the AIDS diagnosis and the thought of entering the apartment, the protective investigation task was taken on by supervisors who, in the absence of medical transport, carried Ms. Morrisey directly to the hospital in an agency car. The hospital, however, flatly refused to admit her, arguing that her condition was chronic, not acute. Yes, they acknowledged she was dying slowly, but so were many other people, such as certain cancer patients. The hospital maintained they could not simply hold such patients until their deaths. Besides, she still owed $150,000 from a previous hospitalization. Ms. Morrisey should be in a nursing home, the hospital insisted—if the agency could find one that was willing to take her.

Agency administrative intervention obtained permission for her entry into a public nursing care facility. However, when word spread quickly that she had AIDS, employees of the facility objected through their union that they were not equipped to care for her and that she should be hospitalized. Additional medical complications, including pneumonia, effected the necessary acute status, which finally led to hospital readmission.

With the mother's admission to the hospital, it was thought that perhaps now the children, who had been quite restless, would stabilize in the aunt's home. However, the opposite was true. The two older boys became more difficult for the aunt to manage. Twice they had run away after claiming to have been beaten; and both times they had run to their mother's friend, Mr. Whitaker. Though she did not know him, the aunt had characterized him as a former drag queen and a participant in the mother's former addicted life.

In fact, Mr. Whitaker was a 24-year-old who had recently married his teenage sweetheart, Rhonda. Both were deeply religious, active participants in a black independent church and demonstrated visible and genuine concern for the welfare of the children and for the mother herself. Mr. Whitaker acknowledged that he had once been part of the street life in his ghetto neighborhood, until he was converted a couple of years before. His religion had given him a new life and he provided character references who could give the agency a more objective description of his reliability and life-style.

Lydia was a poised teenager who possessed a maturity

beyond her 14 years. While most other people avoided her
mother, she visited her regularly and accepted the inevitability
of her death. She held on to a hope that it would not occur for
at least a few years, the maximum time the doctors believed an
AIDS patient could live. We talked, however, about the possibility that death could occur much sooner. Lydia had joined
her two older brothers in the Whitakers' house, and her major
concern, besides her mother's condition, was the fact that the
aunt was trying to keep the two-year-old. She believed that the
aunt wanted to raise him separately from the other siblings.
Lydia wondered if I could help to work this problem out since
her mother was too weak now to struggle with the aunt over
the matter.

When I finally met Ms. Morrisey, in all my medical regalia,
I said I knew I was wearing this strange-looking garb to protect
her from me. She smiled. Though in her late thirties, her face
was drawn and sad; her eyes were not focused properly, and
she appeared emaciated and weak, exhibiting the frailty of an
elderly person. She was tied loosely with a large towel to the
back of her lounge chair to assure that she did not slide out.
There was a spark of interest, however, and sufficient strength
to converse when I mentioned that I had met with three of her
children and with Mr. and Mrs. Whitaker. She was confident
that the Whitakers, though young, would provide an excellent home for all of her children. She would like to have the
children's public assistance checks assigned to the Whitakers,
and she wanted the youngest one to join his siblings right away.
I wrote up a statement covering these points and had her sign
it before witnesses. As the children's legal custodian, the mother
was successful through this means of providing for her children in the best way she knew how.

After attending to these matters and going out of town, I
did not hear from the Morrisey family for several weeks. When
I returned, I called Mr. Whitaker who reported that the hospital had deposited Ms. Morrisey on the doorstep of their new
residence. This abrupt move by the hospital had occurred
about 10 days previous and he said he could not remember
how to reach me. His family had had the good fortune of
acquiring access to a large, attractive, publicly subsidized rental
dwelling. Before they could move into the empty house, how-

ever, an ambulance from the hospital had brought Ms. Morrisey to his new door. She was carried up to the single bedroom on the third floor and left with him. The room was without furniture and was completely bare. Windows without screens opened to the summer heat.

When the community visiting nurse arrived a few days later, she found the patient on a mattress on the floor with flies swarming around her unemptied bedpan. The Whitakers felt very badly that they did not know how to care for her and had neither linens nor basic supplies for doing so. Mr. Whitaker had stayed in the room with Ms. Morrisey for long hours, despite some anxiety about such an exposure. The visiting nurse was understandably appalled and was not at first sure whether to place responsibility upon Mr. Whitaker or the hospital for such conditions. Slowly she began to educate the young couple and Lydia as to the tedious protocols necessary for caring for an AIDS patient. A hospital bed, supplies, and linens were provided a week or so later by a grant from an active AIDS community task force.

The following weeks were stressful for the young family, even though a supportive network was also developing. At this point, I organized a case conference with representatives from the Visiting Nurses Association, the community task force, a homemaker service, and a hospital representative, in order to address a long list of concerns. Mrs. Whitaker also attended this meeting and was relieved to find the beginnings of an organized response to their chaotic situation. At the meeting I also discussed, from a child protective services viewpoint, how the children, though at the Whitakers' home with their mother, must be kept from any exposure to the mother's disease, as through intimate patient care tasks, e.g. taking care of her toilet.

Mr. and Mrs. Whitaker continued to receive excellent instruction from the community nurse and were able to begin to discuss their anxieties and stresses and to accept support from others. Provisions were made for necessary ongoing medical checkups at the hospital. Mr. Whitaker's extended family in the new neighborhood mobilized considerable assistance for the four children.

In the outpatient clinic some weeks later, Ms. Morrisey's

medical checkup indicated a recurrence of pneumonia and other complications which led to her third hospitalization. Because of the outcry over the last very precipitous discharge, the hospital promised to provide at least a week's notice to the family and the service community before discharging her again. Ms. Morrisey remained in the hospital a number of weeks. At the next pre-discharge conference I questioned whether Ms. Morrisey was not again being released quite prematurely and I advocated vigorously for increasing the in-home medical services if discharge were imminent. I was especially concerned that too much had already been demanded of the young couple and of Lydia. Two days before her release, however, Ms. Morrisey's condition suddenly worsened, and she died.

Amid the family's grief there was also a sense of relief that her suffering was finally past. The involved community organizations continued to maintain contact with the family for several months, and the church and extended family as well provided primary comfort and help. During this time, the children found appropriate ways to grieve and adjusted well in their new schools and in the community. Mr. Whitaker and his bride, throughout their ordeal, asserted many times to everyone that "the Lord would surely provide."

Indeed, for this young family there seemed somehow to be no lack of hope for the future.

Chapter 2

THE DANCE BEYOND
THE FAMILY SYSTEM

To recast the family therapist and social worker's roles so that "it is difficult to separate the specialist in 'emotional' problems from the specialist in 'community' problems" is not a new challenge.[1,2] Since this bold admonition was pronounced 20 years ago, systems thinking has revolutionized clinical therapy, creating a flourishing literature and a breadth of family therapy schools. The broader vision of the family in community and the systemic entanglements of these multisystems has, on the other hand, produced a sparse but growing body of knowledge and written material. The family's dependency upon helping agent networks is especially evident in the child welfare realm. Family-centered services have developed as a concept and as a means to strengthen the family's internal functioning, as well as the family's ability to relate effectively to powerful public agents.[3,4]

Social agencies which often refer families for clinical treatment, children and family services, courts, schools, mental hospitals, or day programs, often unwittingly create negatively charged triangulated relationships requiring direct and conjoint communication and case treatment planning.[5,6] Internal conflict among the helping agents of delinquency control is believed to be a contributing factor in the maintenance or exacerbation of delinquent behavior.[7-9] Similarly, a child's experiences in the different environments of the family and the school can at times create contextual and relational dissonances which necessitate intervention into the adult relationships of both settings in order to promote the child's development.[10-12]

A full systems therapeutic approach, therefore, widens the lens of assessment and intervention beyond the family system to the interactive patterns of the family's immediate community and service systems as well. The dance of the various parties is clearly observable and demonstrates that the service community network relationships clearly impact upon treatment outcomes. Since the dysfunctional extrafamilial processes may serve to maintain, exacerbate, or create symptomatic behaviors, it seems neither helpful nor accurate to characterize the interchange as an outgrowth of family pathology, but rather to understand the multisystem interactions as interdependent and contributing.

Assessment characteristics of the interactional process of the family in community suggests at least four rather common dysfunctional modes. The blind or dispersed system operates in a vacuum of disengagement, abdicating responsibility and control. The conflicted interinstitutional system usually sets up a pattern of triangulation in which the family suffers setbacks. The rejecting system is characterized by ideological bias, struggles for reimbursement, or overwhelmed states of operation which create discontinuity and provoke a family's feelings of being cast about. Finally, the underdeveloped system affords the practitioner an opportunity to create optimal, reliable referrals which are coordinated through active conferencing.

THE BLIND SERVICE NETWORK

The seemingly blind service network is composed of dispersed service entities which deal with the client in a manner that demonstrates little or no knowledge of each other's involvements. The client controls the information flow and finds that he/she can reduce factors that might produce change by misinforming or not informing the network of various behaviors. Some important service or monitoring parties will have very little contact with the client because they feel overwhelmed by large caseloads. The more active service participants will feel impotent and wonder why their well-intended work is not favorably influencing the client. An illusion that there is no substantial problem may also operate. The client's defense mechanisms will exploit the service network's detachment, until at some point of desperation, symptomatic behavior will escalate. In sum, the professionals have allowed their own distraction or seduction.

The Oakley family demonstrates classic roles of child and spousal abuse. The alcoholic and suspicious husband, after gaining control over his parenting conduct, became increasingly prone to violence toward his wife. Mrs. Oakley's lack of differentiation and threatened position seemed to cripple her from taking sufficient protective action for herself. Perhaps she also feared the engagement of protective services which could potentially remove the child. Because the father's original attack on the child had been life-threatening, criminal charges led to his prosecution and three years of reporting probation. The abused child was moved for six months to the grandparents' home in another city.

During the first year of probation, Mr. Oakley told his probation officer and the child protective social worker that he was faithfully attending a counseling program and that he was no longer drinking. He was proud of carrying two part-time jobs and that his wife was employed. On the other hand, the wife, frightened and intimidated by her husband, believed that the therapy was making him worse. Indeed, on those days on which he alleged program attendance, he returned home more agitated and more threatening than ever, which led to his wife's secret call to the child protective worker that she was contemplating a move into a women's shelter.

The child protective worker's and supervisor's alarm over the wife's fear of danger prompted an urgent case meeting with the probation officer, therapist, child protective worker, supervisor and, subsequently, with Mr. Oakley. It became quite clear to all of the professionals at their first meeting that indeed their own lack of communication with each other had contributed to the illusion that the client was improving. The therapist had accepted the client's cordiality and persistent denial of drinking and other problems and had agreed to monthly rather than weekly meetings. Until the spousal crisis occurred, the child protective worker had believed that there was little reason to be in contact with the therapist. The probation officer, with a caseload of nearly 250 clients, had not had time to monitor the client closely or to verify his treatment attendance claims. In short, each of the parties had operated in a vacuum with little knowledge of the other's existence, and without an understanding of each other's professional roles in relation to the client family. Indeed, involvement with the family had been sporadic and minimal.

As a result of the case meeting, clinical therapeutic goals and service objectives were developed by the interagency representatives to include: (1) strengthening the wife's status and concept of self, (2) enabling the wife to be in frequent communication with the support system, (3) regular reporting by the therapist to the probation officer, (4) further psychological testing and utilization of a new, intensive group for battering husbands, and (5) holding ongoing case conferences at about six-week intervals to assess progress and further interventions, including consideration of a detoxification program and marital counseling.

While there had been some initial concern that Mr. Oakley might react to the professional system's tighter controls through spousal violence or threats to his wife, it became clear that, instead, his symptomatic behavior was for the first time decreasing. Indeed, a correlation was evident in this case between the incidence of acting-out behavior on the part of the family and the professional community's ability to coordinate its own communication and intervention in an effective way.

THE CONFLICTED SERVICE NETWORK

The conflicted service network is characterized by overt, often intransigent ideological and actual service battles in relation to the client. The client will experience varying degrees of triangulation by the parties who direct or support the client toward divergent goals. The splitting of service participants among themselves or by the client effectively eliminates the achievement of change and maintains the status quo. Differing values concerning maintaining family life vs. placement or institutionalization frequently arouse such systemic conflict. In court-related cases, such as child protective ones, an adversarial position may be unavoidable. When opposing parties are in a fiscal contract with each other, higher executive intervention may help resolve problems. If problem-solving efforts fail, a new and more compatible configuration of service participants will be necessary, along with projection of a period of time gauged to overcome setbacks and psychological damage to the family.

In the Wilson case, a single-parent mother demonstrated toward her son behaviors fluctuating from angry physical assaults to extreme disengagement and depression. Mrs. Wilson demanded that the boy, age 13, change his problematic behaviors, in this instance, stealing at home, acting out at school, and running away. Her practice of overwhelming him with orders and ultimatums and punishment through withdrawal and emotional distancing contributed to his chaotic and volatile behaviors. For the sake of her own coping, she demanded within the family system and service system the absolute right to engage or disengage at will. This behavior expressed itself particularly around placement issues.

Over several years, the mother, with her son intermittently in placement, participated in a number of therapeutic attempts with a range of separate therapists, who were invited to operate quite independently with the family, apart from the service and legal network. The mother sought constantly to bring her son back home from placement at the times when he demonstrated the most progress away from home. She logically asserted that now he was improved or "well" and she could manage him. A recommendation from her therapist coupled with a plea from her attorney completed the triangulation with the placement facility and the child protective agency, setting in motion a judicial system which awarded the mother her child with little consideration for whether or not the mother's relationship with the boy had actually changed.

A systems treatment modality was then instituted to bring together the service planning in the context of family treatment. The child would remain in placement while the family attended biweekly sessions. At least monthly, key service personnel or legal representatives would be brought into sessions to monitor progress and to work cooperatively, if possible, toward the timing of another reunification attempt. The approach was embraced by the family's legal representatives, the current placement social worker, and choreographed by the family therapist and systems case manager from the child protective agency.

A major setback to this new and positive momentum occurred, however, when the original placement agency social worker moved from the agency and was replaced by a new and quite inexperienced worker who promoted an agenda of his own. Observing the newly emerging strengths of the family, and to meet his administrator's strong demands for another bed in the short-term placement center, the new placement social worker operated outside of the framework of the treatment team. Effectively he disrupted the therapeutic environment by allying with the mother's and son's very transitory desire for reunification through a highly premature placement discharge and return home. Opposing the recommendations of the therapist and child protective case manager, Mrs. Wilson sided with the placement agency's social worker, setting in motion again the old negative dynamics of the family. Higher level administrative intervention was not available to mediate the team's conflict, and the team consequently sustained a prolonged and serious setback in relationship to each other and to this mother and son.

When such a split occurs in the interagency team effort, the family's original and maladaptive dynamics will prevail to the client's detriment. The family, having been challenged either through its voluntary or involuntary involvement to try new, constructive behaviors, finds that it is now able to exploit or to be exploited by the irrational dynamics of the service system which had been defined as "helper." The family's inherent difficulties are thus reinforced, making future treatment efforts all the more difficult.

The Rejecting System

When a system is first and foremost responsive to its own operational needs and unresponsive to a client's specific concerns, the client not surprisingly experiences a sense of rejection. The service system may be overwhelmed with too high a volume of work, or it may be anxious about the possibility of not being paid either by the client or the client's insurance. In the large public sector considerable case turnover, e.g., movement of a case from intake to a series of other specialized services, or from worker to worker, disallows sufficient opportunity for individual acquaintance and therapeutic bonds to develop between the counselor and client. Time gaps without service may also exist during transfers of staff. These factors contribute to the maintenance of problematic behaviors and hold the client in the system over extended periods of time. If the client family demonstrates considerable emotional distress, the discontinuous transactions will usually cause an escalation of problems into emergency situations, as the client seeks to reengage rejecting parties or elements of the service. Poorly planned discharges from mental health institutions provide tragic examples, on a massive scale, of rejected, deteriorating patients. Similar phenomena are occurring all too frequently with children's services, health care, aging, and other services as well.

In the Morrisey case (see Chapter 1), a single-parent mother and former drug abuser, suffering from AIDS, was denied readmittance to a large metropolitan hospital largely because of an enormous outstanding bill, not yet covered by medical assistance.

The family's grief extended not only to the mother's misery and imminent death, but to the rejecting treatment of this modern health care and social service system. Counseling was effective in large part because it acknowledged the social system's dysfunction as a key component of the traumatic and tragic circumstances. The practitioner intervened to help organize case conferences with hospital personnel, the community nursing system, a community-based AIDS task force, and a homemaker service. Stabilization of the turbulent system enabled the family to better focus upon Ms. Morrisey's and their own needs and to appropriately grieve at her death when it occurred.

In summary, the rejecting nature and disarray of the original service system greatly contributed to an increase of stress and dysfunction in this family. The original health problem was exacerbated as another family member became abusive and two of the children in turn began to run away. This escalation likewise provided another signal for help by the extended family after their earlier, more rational protestations had fallen on deaf ears. An empathetic professional response developed finally out of the reorganized service community. This development led to a rather rapid, yet lasting, amelioration of the situation of the extended family members, as the health needs of the mother and the caretaking needs of the children were jointly resolved by the multiple professional parties, who had now begun to communicate with each another on behalf of the entire family. The formal joint meetings of the various services organized by the social worker provided a setting for public accountability and advocacy, which reduced the rejecting tendency of the original services.

THE UNDERDEVELOPED SYSTEM

It is not uncommon to discover with socially isolated families, or with families new to the service system, significant cultural deprivation, including an absence of key service providers. A careful systems-oriented therapeutic intake process for a client will, therefore, determine the client's current range and degree of involvement within the service community. These parties may include schools, health centers, doctors, legal personnel, religious institutions, etc.

Since the inexperienced client may also feel insecure around professionals and be easily overwhelmed, the client needs a good deal of support in establishing an effective network and in following through after professional contacts have begun. It is essential that the systems practitioner know the referral resources as well. A personal call, accompanying the client, or inviting the other professionals into sessions provides a clear and visible means to establish interagency team relationships. There is also nothing more unhelpful to such a client than to refer him/her to unresponsive or inappropriate sources. Careful preparation including role-play and agenda-setting prepares the client for successful relationships with the network. Crisis points may be the most likely times to establish the coordinated services.

Ms. Reland (see also Chapter 3), a mother in her early twenties, entered the service network involuntarily through a child protective report and investigation. Her relative isolation had been a contributing factor to her frustration with and physical abuse of her six-year-old son, Timmy. She was also burdened by the demands of an active four-year-old daughter. Although she felt at first quite defensive toward the protective service agency, claiming that she was being harassed, she responded with interest and a sense of relief when advocacy was offered around Timmy's acknowledged school problems. She had had several unsuccessful encounters with a punitive principal and was understandably distressed that Timmy was so frequently suspended from school. The school, she felt, was not dealing with Timmy or his problems and had alienated her as well. Illiterate and quite simple in her speech and manner, Ms. Reland was ready to readdress Timmy's school problems with the assistance of an advocate.

The development of new and functioning relationships within the school system also provided opportunities for building trust and rapport between the client and worker. Based upon this relationship with the client, a second referral was initiated, this time to a clinical therapist and educational treatment program. In this instance the systems worker selected a source personally known, and attended the initial session in order to introduce the client to the new therapist and to clarify treatment goals. The clinical intake process revealed that Timmy had been conceived through a rape incident which had contributed to his mother's very negative, vindictive attitude toward him.

While the therapist's relationship developed, the social worker, operating as a team member with the therapist, linked the client family to additional services as needs were identified. These services included a day-care program for the four-year-old girl and, later, a family shelter for the mother and her children, when she moved out of her own home to avoid abuse from her paramour. The therapist also extended the network by arranging for an educational specialist to work with each child, and for a case conference with Timmy's teacher. Joint efforts of the therapist and social worker promoted the client's emotional development and a system of tangible supports in the community. In summary, the client's isolation and abusive behaviors were mitigated through the client's engagement with an evolving supportive treatment and service community.

CONCLUSION

From an ecological systems perspective, the behavioral patterns of the family may be linked directly with those of the service system providers. This linkage may be profound, particularly in cases where the family's acting out has violated social norms, requiring powerful interventions from society, e.g., adult criminal justice, child welfare, juvenile justice, and mental health systems, or where a family member may be exceedingly vulnerable, as in the health care context. As if dealing with a series of powerful parental figures, the client, after the initial intervention, must reckon with the accountable presence, for better or worse, of various, and often multiple service personnel. Further dysfunctional family behavior may be correlated with the patterns, often irrational, of the complex service system itself.

How well the service community network recognizes their joint existence and influence in relationship to the family will greatly impact upon treatment and service effectiveness. The blind, triangulated, or rejecting service configurations are particularly apt to invite from certain families an escalation and reenforcement of presenting difficulties. On the other hand, the awareness by the service personnel of each other as a potentially supportive community provides an essential context for positive change in the family.

Finally, while there has been some cross-fertilization among the related service fields and some broadening of clinical social work roles, in particular, during the 1980's, the frontier that combines individual, family, and social systems assessment and operations into a sophisticated joint practice continues to remain open for active exploration. Families with serious problems, also intertwined in the dysfunctional social web, can only benefit from such systems' expansionary approaches.

Chapter 3

A DIFFERENT PLACE
A Vignette

The following vignette, "A Different Place," depicts a young, very poor, and rather isolated mother who physically abused her son. Through active and comprehensive treatment, the client's development occurs in four discernible phases. Firstly, from a place of suspicion and angry passive resistance the client begins to trust the child protective social worker as a benevolent force. Secondly, she responds to new modes of communication with the worker which she is taught to utilize with her children. Thirdly, a hidden and abusive spousal relationship is interrupted in the form of an acute housing crisis. Fourthly, the client begins to develop adult autonomy, a more positive sense of identity, and new personal skills. A series of appropriate social services including the school, a family shelter, and a therapeutic and tutoring service are orchestrated by the social worker. This case is discussed from a theoretical service perspective in Chapter 2 and from a psychodynamic/systems therapeutic view in Chapter 10.

No one answered the door. It was the only house on the block whose windows were boarded up. If a neighbor had not confirmed the address and names of the residents one would have assumed the house to be vacant. After several attempts to meet Satie Reland and her two young children at her home, I had finally submitted a petition to the court. Ms. Reland ignored the first mailed subpoena, but arrived in court a few weeks later after a sheriff hand-delivered the second.

We met in the court waiting room. Satie was 5 feet tall and about 50 pounds overweight. She wore a gray, somewhat smudged, quilted coat which fit tightly and seemed to cushion her from an environment which she was certain must be hostile. She was perturbed at being required to attend court. Her speech and questions were, however, quite simple. She was not accustomed to dealing with professionals and had difficulty expressing the anger she felt. Satie wanted to know who kept leaving those letters at her door, and why she was being harassed? She said she might not take her child to a clinic ever again. She did not deny the existence of the old and permanent scars which the doctors had found on her six-year-old Timmy's buttocks, or that she had put them there by beating him. But she was not beating her son now, she said. It had been an old problem and was over. Couldn't we just leave her alone?

I told her I would like to believe her story, but that I would have to know her for a period of time in order to be certain that Timmy was being treated well. Hadn't she told the original investigative worker before my attempted visits that she would be interested in ongoing social services? I said I understood that she must have been surprised and angry with the doctors. After all, she was trying to benefit her child by taking him for a routine checkup and had suddenly been reported and required now to deal with social workers and a judge. I tried to give her at least a little benefit of the doubt. Perhaps it *was* an old problem. I suggested that we meet together with Timmy to discuss how he was getting along and what her concerns were. We could then hope to report to the court in about 6 months about how well Timmy was doing, that he had been monitored, and was not being abused. Ms. Reland agreed to this plan; our mutual goal at this point was to get my agency and the courts off her back!

We met in Satie Reland's home about a week after the court hearing. Despite the abandoned appearance of the outside, the living room was furnished with reasonably comfortable seats and sofas. The electricity was on and, presumably, other utilities. Timmy and his four-year-old sister Alison were curious and eager to meet the visitor. After I had talked a few minutes with the children about their favorite games, Satie placed in my hand a crumpled note which Timmy had brought her today from school. She asked with some embarrassment if I would read it to her, since she could not read well enough to be sure what it said.

Though only in the first grade, Timmy had been suspended by the school principal for 5 days for fighting with another child. I encouraged his mother to ask Timmy directly what had happened. Timmy's reply was halting. Both embarrassed and furious with him, Satie was unwilling to hear him out. Her immediate conclusions were that he was a very bad child, and she told him so in harsh, angry terms. The mother's frustration was considerable and she clearly needed a place to sound off. I was glad that I could be there to take some of the heat for Timmy. He had been her target long enough.

When I suggested that we make a school visit, Ms. Reland was visibly relieved. She acknowledged how exasperated she felt with the principal, whose only solution to problems had been to suspend Timmy repeatedly and then to summon her to school for a lecture. There had already been several confrontations between the principal and herself and Satie felt that she could not deal further with this person. Intervention on this level for Ms. Reland provided our second alliance. She became aware that there was both support and practical follow-up through this service which she had at first thought was there only to harass her.

Over the next few months Timmy continued to create problems at the school which required negotiation and the development of relationships among the adults in his life. A school counselor provided a helpful mediating influence with the principal, who had been both rigid and, at times, belligerent toward the mother. To break the pattern of suspensions we persuaded the principal to send Timmy to the counselor if he became unmanageable in the classroom. Special education was also requested, as Timmy's learning appeared to be quite delayed and he needed a small, structured classroom setting.

In addition, an excellent learning therapy program was available in the community. In our joint initial visit to this program, Satie Reland indicated that she had been raped by a

friend of her family when she was a teenager. Timmy was the
bitter product of that incident, about which she had thus far
talked very little. While Timmy would receive tutoring twice
each week, Ms. Reland would be be able to meet with an older
female counselor, with whom she would, over the next year,
develop an intimate supportive relationship. Satie also acknowledged her own difficulty in reading and her inability to help
Timmy with his homework. After Timmy's stabilization at
school and the enrollment of the younger child, Alison, in
regular day care, the mother's counseling experience provided
her with an opportunity to address deeper issues about her
own identity and development.

Paradoxically, her personal growth precipitated a major
crisis. Satie had moved into an abandoned house several years
ago on an agreement with a city housing agency that she would
bring it up to a habitable standard. Her live-in boyfriend, the
father of the younger child, had been a burden and ongoing threat. He lived off her meager public-assistance income,
drank, abused her at times, and did nothing to improve the
further deteriorating dwelling. She kept his presence and
identity a secret for many months and would not bring this
man into any meetings. As her own self-esteem developed,
however, she abruptly left the man and the house, taking the
children with her.

Because there was not space enough in a cousin's house
for the children and her to stay, they entered a family shelter
in a church. With our encouragement, and with transportation
money provided by the shelter, Satie kept Timmy in his school
program and Alison in her day-care situation during an up-
heaval which lasted for about 10 weeks. The staff in the church
was highly supportive during this period of time. Since private
housing was not affordable, Ms. Reland registered for public
housing, as the various service professionals jointly advocated
the city's housing authority. Eventually, a respectable public
low-rise dwelling was acquired by Ms. Reland, in part because
while in the shelter she had been designated "homeless." This
designation gave priority to her housing request.

By the spring of the year Timmy finally no longer stood
out as the child who was always getting into trouble at the

school. He had settled into a structured, small-group, special-education class and was progressing there and in the learning therapy program which continued in the community. Alison continued to benefit from the day-care program. Satie had learned to communicate with Timmy rather than to vent her rage upon him. She had an ongoing network of persons in the various programs; some were professional helpers, others were newly acquired friends to whom she could turn when frustrated. The protective monitoring/counseling service lasted a little over a year.

The special-education and therapeutic work would continue, from the community programs, for several years. At the first annual review meeting, Satie was clearly a more satisfied and higher-functioning young woman than she had been a year ago. Although she still could not read, she was overcoming many of her defenses around this subject as she actively supported her children's development. She and her children were comfortably settled in a new subsidized apartment. More relaxed, and having lost much of her extra weight, she was emerging as an attractive, quiet, and more confident woman.

Chapter 4

PARENT–SCHOOL–CHILD SYSTEMIC DANCES
Triadic Assessment

Over the past 2 decades a number of sophisticated sociologists and family therapists in their separate fields have developed a new systemic perspective of delinquence and school-related problems. The previous child-centered paradigms were the psychoanalytic view that focused on the child's characterological deficits and the traditional sociological outlook that enumerated the general environmental variables that seemed to produce negative behaviors. The newer systems and interactionists' views maintain, however, that the child's negative conduct is symptomatic of very specific and current malfunctioning sequences of behavior within the child's human network. Therefore, it is important to look not only at the child's actions but also at the behaviors and relationships of the adult actors in the system, especially the parents and helping professionals who relate to the child. Further, the systemic model requires a means of intervention that can then bring together the significant persons of the whole system on behalf of the child.

Although a child's personality and environmental setting indeed have relevance, the interactionist view has convincingly pointed out that specific systems of helping professionals may effectively select and, at times promote certain youth for delinquent careers. Delinqency may not be a special kind of behavior at all, but rather a socially conferred status.[1]

For example, tracking of children in schools or teachers' lowering their expectations of children are practices that often have a negatively self-fulfilling quality. Also, the progressive notion of seeking to remediate all problems, even those that youths would naturally abandon on their own, may exacerbate and prolong difficulties.[2] Indeed, the juvenile justice system through its own internal inconsistencies, whether punitive or rehabilitative in intent, can further promote delinquent careers.[3-6]

Beyond the inherent and complex problems within the juvenile justice and school systems that foster negative performance and behaviors, family therapists have shown that youths who are lodged between strongly competing systems—for example, family, school, peers—may begin to manifest symptomatic conduct. Such actions may, upon examination, ultimately reveal strong conflicts of values and expectations among the adults of the various systems—struggles which are placed upon the child to mediate.[7,8]

METHODOLOGY OF THE STUDY

In order to examine more closely the nature of this intersystems problem and its potential consequences for the child, a piece of exploratory research was conducted by the author in a public child welfare agency. The purpose of the study was to consider the quality and styles of relationships between parents and school personnel and how the interactional patterns of the adults might bear upon youths' behavior in the school setting. The research involved interviews of a small random sample of parents whose public high school children had been referred by the police for truancy. Based on these interviews, assessments were made of the parents' attitudes toward particular school personnel with whom they dealt and their reported responses to the professionals and to their children. Rather than focusing upon the child per se, the study examined the triadic framework in which each child operated, with special focus on the quality of the adult relationships, that

is, of the parents and the school professionals. Three different typologies of parent–school–child interactional systemic
dances emerged from the study, namely, aggressive entanglement, passive entanglement, and the adaptive response.

Aggressive Entanglement

The aggressive entanglement pattern is characterized by
overtly hostile behaviors on the part of the school and the
parents, coupled with the parents' nondiscerning alliance with
the child. As the school initiates behaviors toward the child or
parents which the parents consider to be highly unfavorable,
the parents respond in kind with active and increasingly critical
behaviors toward the school. An escalation pattern develops as
the child continues behaviors at school that cannot be sanctioned by the school system.

In one sense, the child is caught in the middle of conflicting adult relationships. He or she may indeed be the communication bearer, sometimes awkwardly positioned in the crossfire
of the adults, as seen in the example in which an angry principal tells the child, "Tell your mother I want to see her at
school!" Similarly, the school's acknowledged use of suspensions as a "means to get the parents into the school" puts the
child in the potentially damaging situation of being the communication link between the school and the parents.

From a paradoxical perspective, the child's overt defiances
at school may become a means of activating the adults of both
systems to resolve a particular problem and their conflicting
standards for the child. As the child acts out at school, he or
she may also be riding on the shoulders of the parents in their
disagreement with the school.

For instance, a mother in the study reported that she had
argued for several years with the principal over the school's
failure to provide the necessary programs that would meet her
son's needs and thereby inspire him to attend school regularly
and to behave acceptably. A sense of significant negative emotional involvement on the part of the mother with the principal

was noted in her descriptions of the situation. This mother, with what appeared to be some legitimate school complaints, had nevertheless become locked over a period of time into an argumentative pattern with the principal. She believed that the school's rules were rigid and unfair, and she argued that she could not support them. Furthermore, she would not seek behavioral changes in her son, who was acting out, "until his educational needs are met." Thereby she struggled *through the child* against an equally "hard-nosed" principal.

Although the child had considerable manipulative power, he was also awkwardly positioned between a parent and principal who would not compromise. In some serious ways he was victimized in the triadic relationship; for example, the school refused to permit the child to take the school's shop course. The mother also felt that "he had been labeled as a behavior problem" and thereby was more readily tagged for disciplinary procedures. Indeed, he had been suspended a number of times for seemingly trivial reasons such as walking in the hallways during classtime, being late to school, or not carrying his picture identification.

An escalating entanglement pattern developed as the mother became increasingly angry and unsupportive of the school with each incident. She appeared to be in a kind of "game without end," a repetitive cycle in which her efforts to defend her son from the injustices of the school either victimized him further or gave him an implied license to maintain his rebellious conduct. Sadly, this mother reported that her son finally received a disciplinary transfer for cursing at a teacher when told to remove his hat. This type of transfer would move the problem and the parent out of the neighborhood school to a socially segregated disciplinary school where *all* of the children were labeled as serious discipline problems.

Another example of this aggressive entanglement pattern is that of a mother whose high-school daughter reported regularly that she was being picked on by a reading teacher. The parent sided with her daughter's claim rather quickly and unequivocally. When the teacher called the parent on the phone, a hostile conversation ensued, and the mother recommended without success that her daughter be permitted to transfer to another teacher. The mother became further upset that this teacher "will not let go." The child continued to report being picked on, and a second call came from the department head, also resulting in an unresolved argument.

In the course of the interview, the mother acknowledged that her daughter had had similar problems with other teachers in previous years and had tended to "fly off" at them. The mother concluded her description of the problem with the acknowledgment that "perhaps I need a mediator to help sort out this problem."

In sum, the aggressively entangled relationship is characterized by conflicting demands between the parent and the school (see Fig. 4-1). Sides are drawn and hostile interchanges occur without progress or resolution. The child has the almost unconditional support of the parent and is either accused of or precipitates behaviors at school that are not sanctioned. The parent feels that the child is unfairly labeled as a behavior problem and is subsequently tagged for reprimand or exaggerated punishments by the school. Ultimately, the child suffers directly as he or she may drop out of school, be pushed out (disciplinary transfer or multiple suspensions), or may remain in school but exhibit problematic conduct.

Passive Entanglement

Similar to aggressively entangled parents, the passively entangled parents are also stalemated in positions that are in conflict with school personnel. These parents, however, are less willing to enter into extended conflicts with the school; instead they gradually withdraw and tend to permit their children to miss school. These parents usually report that they have made frustrated attempts to resolve the problems with the school, but now feel that the situation is hopeless. In short, they give up, and again it is the children who lose in the three-way struggle (see Fig. 4-2).

For instance, parents in the study often felt that they were being given bureaucratic runarounds and not being taken

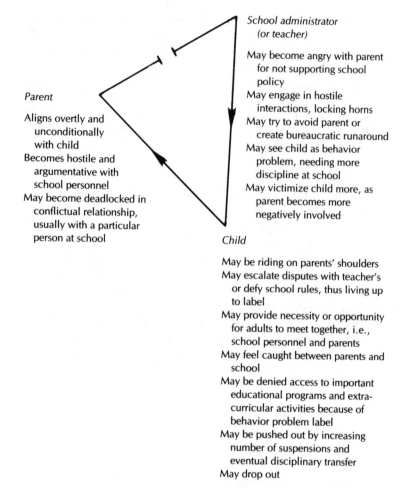

Figure 4-1. Aggressive entanglement.

School administrator
(or teacher)

May become angry with parent
for not supporting school
policy
May engage in hostile
interactions, locking horns
May try to avoid parent or
create bureaucratic runaround
May see child as behavior
problem, needing more
discipline at school
May victimize child more, as
parent becomes more
negatively involved

Parent

Aligns overtly and
unconditionally
with child
Becomes hostile and
argumentative with
school personnel
May become deadlocked in
conflictual relationship,
usually with a particular
person at school

Child

May be riding on parents' shoulders
May escalate disputes with teacher's
or defy school rules, thus living up
to label
May provide necessity or opportunity
for adults to meet together, i.e.,
school personnel and parents
May feel caught between parents and
school
May be denied access to important
educational programs and extra-
curricular activities because of
behavior problem label
May be pushed out by increasing
number of suspensions and
eventual disciplinary transfer
May drop out

seriously in their early requests for help. A parent reported with strong feeling that her son was not academically inclined and should be learning a trade or practical skills at school. Her comment about conferences with the principal and later with the counselors was, "They talked, and I listened." After making several trips to the school, she finally concluded, "The school

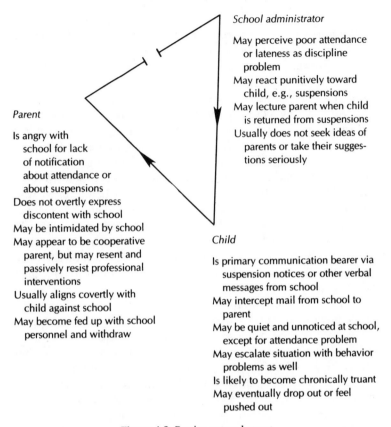

School administrator

May perceive poor attendance
    or lateness as discipline
    problem
May react punitively toward
    child, e.g., suspensions
May lecture parent when child
    is returned from suspensions
Usually does not seek ideas of
    parents or take their sugges-
    tions seriously

Parent

Is angry with
    school for lack
    of notification
    about attendance or
    about suspensions
Does not overtly express
    discontent with school
May be intimidated by school
May appear to be cooperative
    parent, but may resent and
    passively resist professional
    interventions
Usually aligns covertly with
    child against school
May become fed up with school
    personnel and withdraw

Child

Is primary communication bearer via
    suspension notices or other verbal
    messages from school
May intercept mail from school to
    parent
May be quiet and unnoticed at school,
    except for attendance problem
May escalate situation with behavior
    problems as well
Is likely to become chronically truant
May eventually drop out or feel
    pushed out

Figure 4-2. Passive entanglement.

doesn't have anything to offer." Tiring of the unsatisfactory situation, she then allied with her son in his desire to miss school, with the defense, "He doesn't just sit around the house but stays active." Then, with resignation, she added, "He is just wasting time at home until he's sixteen and can go to trade school."

A second example is a mother who reported that as a part of a small racial minority her son had been threatened by the other youngsters on the school bus. On behalf of her son she sought transfers to a more integrated and closer annex of the same school, which would also place him within walking distance of home. She felt that her concerns for adult supervision on the buses were not taken seriously, and that the vice-principal had continually blocked her requests for transfers. She was quite angry that the school was so inflexible when it clearly had the option of allowing the boy to transfer to the other annex. However, she became tired of struggling, and finally colluded with the boy by allowing him to remain out of school. She reported, in addition, that she had had a similar problem involving an older son, who eventually dropped out of school.

A complex and in many ways more disturbing extension of the passive triadic interactional pattern is characterized by parents who give the outward appearance of being allied with the school against the child because of their own ambivalence or their lack of assertive skills in an intimidating situation. In fact, the conflict between the parents and the school personnel remains submerged, undoubtedly to the confusion of the child involved, who may feel both supported and unsupported in a contradictory manner.

In this type of situation, the youth also may escalate negative behaviors at school, providing with each incident an opportunity or necessity for clarification by the parents and school officials as to their expectations and, ultimately, his or her future in the school. These parents may feel intimidated, overburdened, and hassled by a series of unsuccessful professional interventions. While the parents take an outwardly cooperative stance, they may harbor unacknowledged resentment both toward the series of professionals involved and toward their own child.

For instance, a parent in the study reported that she was quite upset to have received her first notification of her son's attendance problem only after it had become quite serious. In addition, this notification had come from the district-level home and school visitor rather than from the local school, where it should have originated. A court case on the truancy matter followed, which the mother considered to be educationally interruptive because the youth missed additional days from school each time the hearing was postponed or continued. Although the mother was distressed, she was too intimidated to complain to the local school or to the court.

In this conflictual context, the boy's initial problem advanced from poor attendance to "bad" behavior when he was at school. The mother's first visit to the school occurred at this point as a result of a 5-day suspension placed on the boy for allegedly fighting. The mother believed the boy's story that he had been jumped by several other youths, and was not at fault; indeed, she corroborated the story with the homeroom teacher. What appeared at first to be a supportive intervention on the part of the parent changed, however, to a negative stance as a teacher convinced her that the boy was a class clown. A meeting with the principal and the mother also took a negative direction, and the mother was not assertive enough to question the propriety of the original 5-day suspension. From the mother's report it would seem that she left both meetings with the problem unresolved and with her own conflict with the school personnel submerged. Also, no attempts were made to consider the youth's social or educational needs.

Unfortunately, and perhaps not surprisingly, the boy then allegedly stole a wallet at school. New court hearings for delinquency began at this point, resulting in the boy's missing more school days for continued court appearances. The probation officer became involved and tried unsuccessfully to motivate the youth. In a traditional manner, the problem continued to be seen as belonging exclusively to the boy, and there was no substantial involvement by the probation officer with the parent or with any school personnel.

In sum, this parent felt she had been informed too late of her son's absences, that the school had offered no help in resolving the problems at school, and that she and her son were essentially harassed by two court cases and by school suspensions that kept him out of school even more. The series of professionals involved focused upon the child as a "truant," "the class clown," "a behavior problem," "a delinquent," and finally as a "dropout." It is a common and perhaps classic example of a child who is caught in a context of conflicting adults and who acquires and then lives up to the labels imposed by the system. With the inability of the professionals and the parent to reach or even to seek a collaborative understanding of the youth's educational and social needs, a progression of increasingly serious behaviors was demonstrated by the youth himself.

It is noteworthy that the parents of both of these response

categories find themselves in similar school contexts and having similar problems with school personnel. The aggressively entangled parent maintains an ongoing and more openly hostile response to the school's alienating procedures, resulting in escalating, negative experiences for the child at school. On the other hand, the passively entangled parent seems to despair of the school personnel, and *of the school as a whole*. This parent gives up the struggle, leading to long-term truancy and probable dropout by the youngster.

ADAPTIVE RESPONSE

In contrast to the two dysfunctional interactional dances that have been described, a more adaptive response model was also suggested by the study (see Fig. 4-3). While the complaints of the parents in this group were fairly similar to those of the other typologies with regard to how they were initially treated by school personnel, the adaptive parents found effective ways of coping and were able to circumvent the destructive entanglement cycles.

Moreover, the adaptive parents seemed to be able to distinguish between the school's flaws and its strengths. While they complained strongly about similar types of school problems (inappropriate and rigid suspension and lateness policies, condescending ways in which they were treated), they were less likely to lose all hope in the school or to become stalemated in the unproductive triadic patterns. Rather than becoming embroiled in conflict or passively resigned, they persevered and seemed to demonstrate more sophisticated negotiating or maneuvering skills.

For example, a mother registered her very strong disapproval of the school's rigid lateness and class-cutting policies which had resulted in several suspensions for her child. While the mother was quite frustrated in her attempts to address these issues with the local school administrators, she reported favorably on her experiences with some of the teachers in the school. As she took the child's class-cutting problem around the

INITIAL PHASE: CONFLICTUAL
Parent

Tries to articulate needs
If not "heard" or respected,
  may feel angry or
  intimidated

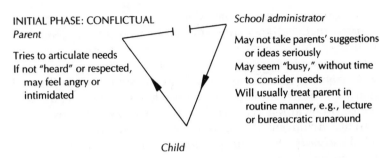

School administrator

May not take parents' suggestions
  or ideas seriously
May seem "busy," without time
  to consider needs
Will usually treat parent in
  routine manner, e.g., lecture
  or bureaucratic runaround

Child

Confused by school policies and treatment
May experiment with negative behaviors at school
  or continue poor attendance

SECOND PHASE: PERSISTENCE

School administrator

Eventually decides parent is a
  "concerned parent"
Concedes to some of parent's
  demands

Parent

May make a number of
  visits to school until
  resolution is reached
  with administrator, e.g.,
  school to call parent
  rather than a suspension
Sees that child's needs are recognized

Child

May begin to get educational needs
  met and perform better

POSSIBLE THIRD PHASE:
  CIRCUMVENTION*

*Teacher (or other school-related
  official)*
May respond to parent favorably
May intervene with administrator
Will work with parent and child
  toward solutions

Parent

Resolves issues with
  someone else in system

Child

Is no longer communication bearer
Is clearer about adult expectations

*If adaptive parents are unable to resolve difficulties at second phase, they will usually seek out
another school-related official (e.g., teacher, counselor) who is sympathetic and helpful.

Figure 4-3. Adaptive model.

administrators to the teacher whose class was being missed, she learned that the boy's stuttering problem was being exhibited in oral reading exercises before the class. The teacher had not been aware of the degree of the youth's embarrassment, and after consulting with the parent and the youth, it was decided that he could read aloud to the teacher privately. The attendance problem was resolved in this coordinated manner as the parent circumvented the punitive attitudes of the school's administrators that had previously served to maintain the problem.

In another instance, a father had become upset with the administrator of the school for suspending his son for attendance problems, a response by the school which he felt the child himself wanted. After a number of visits to the school, this active father finally reached an informal agreement with the school office that he would be called directly whenever his son did not show up for school. Also, an experienced home and school visitor responded to the youth's interest in working in the afternoons and was able to find him a job and to obtain the approval of the school officials and the father. The youth began to attend school regularly, and worked as well.

Some parents were indeed able to move beyond initial conflicts with the school and to find solutions. These persevering parents seemed to better understand the complexity of the problems and placed some responsibility for changes upon themselves or upon the child. In one case, a mother indicated that she herself was in error, as she had permitted her daughter to stay home because of an asthmatic condition, but later in the day had allowed her to go shopping, during which time the daughter was stopped by the police for truancy.

The parents in this group also found somewhat broader ways of defining the problem. While they may have been upset with some school officials, they did not turn against the school as a whole. Rather, they were able to assertively pursue the concerns of their children. For example, at least two very persistent parents reported that after four or five visits to the school, they reached agreements with the dean of boys that he would call them first if a problem occurred, rather than simply suspend their children.

Sometimes these parents were able to go beyond the administrative level and to work with teachers directly. In one case, a parent was able to find helpful assistance at a child guidance clinic, and in another case, a parent felt that the home and school visitor had helped to negotiate a solution for his son's school problem with the school counselor. In short, these parents were able to work with other adults in the system, relieving the child from the awkward role of communication bearer. In each of these cases the child's problem behavior (usually lateness or truancy) ended as the adults (i.e., parents and school personnel) established working communication with one another. The remarkable fact is that the communication occurred in spite of what many parents considered to be serious initial roadblocks from the school's administration and rigid attendance policies.

SUMMARY

Table 4-1, "Key Characteristics of Parents in Reference to the School Personnel" provides a comparative overview of the three primary styles discussed in this chapter. It is noteworthy that all of the parents experienced rather similar frustrations in their initial dealings with the school; and there was a general sense of resentment toward overly punitive and rigid policies and practices of the school, especially in relation to attendance matters.

In terms of actual number of contacts with the school, the passively entangled parents seemed to have the least, unless, however, the child became involved with the court system, thereby bringing in the involvement of another hierarchy of professionals, each of which was increasingly removed from the original school-related issues. Behaviorally, this type of parent may, because of intimidation, appear to be cooperative; however, he/she is usually unable to articulate the needs of the child. Though at times colluding with the denunciatory behaviors of the school officials, the parent is covertly allied with the child—a stance which is undoubtedly confusing for the child.

Table 4-1. Key Characteristics of Parents in Reference to School Personnel

Characteristic	Timing/frequency	Attitude toward school personnel	Style of contact	Attitude toward youth	Response of school to parent	Outcome for child
Passive	Minimal contact First contact may be with "home and school visitor" May take child to school after suspensions May avoid contact	Resentful that local school has not notified them promptly May feel hassled by professionals Mistrustful and has lost hope in schools	Does not express disapproval Tries a few times and quits May be intimidated May appear to be cooperative parent May not respond to outreach interventions	Usually covertly allied with child Publicly may blame child May resent child for causing hassles	Local school usually neglects to notify and contact parent May lecture parent on parenting Bureaucratic run-around Too busy to listen or interpret needs	Educational neglect Grade retention Punitive of attendance problem May suspend for lateness or class cutting Child may become truant/dropout
Aggressive	Parent brings child back frequently after suspensions May have more contact, including	Feels that administration is rigid and unfair Feels that school is victimizing child	May become hostile or argumentative Strongly defensive of child and accusatory of school	Overtly allied with child against school Readily believes all of child's reports	Neglects to notify parents May lock horns with parent May seek to avoid	Negative behaviors may escalate at school Child may acquire serious negative

	telephone/letters	unduly Sees school as whole as having nothing to offer and damaging	May become deadlocked in battle with particular school personnel		parent and send elsewhere	label Many suspensions (or a transfer) May push out youth or promote drop-out Needs unassessed
Adaptive	Parent returns child to school after suspensions Persists with administrators May seek sympathetic school person Visits teachers and may seek professional aid	May see some school personnel as rigid and unfair Distinguishes between personnel who are helpful or not Feels that the schools have some valid programs	May express negative views to school May become angry Can also have polite dialogue If stalemated will seek out someone who can help	Distinguishes between child's possibly negative involvement and school's rigidity and unfairness Supportive of child but will also challenge child	If convinced parent is concerned school may agree to phone parent regularly May eventually provide resources & programs May work with parent and other professionals for a solution	Child may test situation with nonsanctioned behaviors Child copes or settles down May receive testing and assistance with needs; sometimes creative solutions

When the more passively inclined parent makes gestures of support for the child, he/she usually experiences as a part of the triadic interactional cycle the condescending or discrediting behaviors from the school personnel. As the child maintains or escalates the non-sanctioned conduct, the parent becomes increasingly frustrated both with the school and with the child. As we have seen, children in large bureaucratically designed schools can then become easily subjected to systemic neglect. Their needs are not addressed and in time they may drop out, or feel that they are pushed out of the school.

While the more passively inclined parent has less frequent contact, the aggressively entangled parent has a number of sporadic episodes with the school. Feeling that the school is being unfair both in its treatment to the child and to themselves, this parent may do battle with a particular school official. More commonly, there is an ongoing struggle with an administrator or a teacher. This parent takes a position of overt alliance with the child and, believing the child to be victimized, he/she takes on the child's battle. Angry with the parent for supporting the child's infractions, the school personnel may further label and punish the child, thereby reinforcing the parents' original accusations of victimization. A stalemated game without end occurs, which is quite damaging to the child, who may, as the result of severe or ongoing incidents, be pushed out of the school via a disciplinary transfer or some other means. The child may have considerable manipulative control in this type of system, but is also caught between the adults as the communication bearer.

Lastly, the adaptive parents are less likely to become stalemated. Like the other parents, they may have real grievances; however, these parents tend to persist more actively and constructively until they obtain at least some support or recognition for their child's needs. They seem to have the skills which enable them to maneuver better around the roadblocks of the school system, as they seek out someone in it who can help them with the problem. They are more open to professional interventions and may, in fact, seek services. These parents list more contributing factors or reasons for the problem than the others; and while they may be supportive of the child, they also challenge his/her behavior if it seems to be inappropriate. With time, the school administrators seem to develop respect for this parent as a concerned parent, and there may be a resulting readier access for the child to needed resources and services. Though critical of the school, these parents usually indicate that it has some good programs to offer, as well.

Therefore, in all three typologies, the mutual interaction of the parent and the school personnel appears to play a significant role in both the favorable and unfavorable outcomes for the child. The next theoretical chapter (Chapter 6) will analyze successful professional methods of intervention into the problematic triadic parent–school–child system.

Chapter 5

"LOSING HIS TURN"
A Vignette

Everyone else in the Kelly family was placed in an institution at some point by the father. Indeed, his wife, with alcoholic and psychotic behaviors, had several hospitalizations before deserting the family many years ago. Subsequently, the three teenage daughters entered a Catholic group home, and Darrell, at 16, was moved to a drug rehabilitation program. Now Danny, 13, was soon to have his turn. According to the case record, Mr. Kelly, who seemed to thrive on chaos, continually abdicated his parental role by sabotaging all straightforward professional efforts to assist him with his children's out-of-control behaviors, especially their drug abuse, truancy, and petty thefts. The new family-oriented service approach therefore called for developing rapport with him and at the same time subtly taking charge by creating a legitimate crisis beyond his control.

The framing of the placement question therefore was not whether Danny should enter child placement, i.e., "having his turn like all the rest," but what kind of placement and what control the father and son could have in determining the quality of that placement choice. A long-term passive entanglement between the father and son with the school system accounted for two complete years of truancy. Paradoxically, in preparing for a good placement alternative, the parent was challenged to resolve the school attendance problem with the boy. This effort would ultimately determine whether Danny could succeed in the community or not. This vignette illustrates the parent–school–child dance in conjunction with carefully coordinated court and social service interventions. The social worker's relationship was both authoritative and nurturant.

43

Of course, everyone liked Mr. Kelly. He had grown up in this neighborhood where people still stopped on the streets to talk to each other about their children, to chat about the weather, or to relive last night's high school ballgame. Mr. Kelly was usually quite cheerful with his neighbors, although everyone also knew about his "big troubles" and carefully shied away from these subjects—at least to his face.

If people wanted information they could obtain it from him at Marty's Pub. Among his many short-lived jobs, Mr. Kelly had tried bartending there for a while. He remarked that bartenders really do listen to everyone else's woes and he admitted that he was indeed consoled by even worse stories he heard about *other* people's lives.

But Mr. Kelly did not just listen to others' tragic tales. He also shared his story, at times with relish—the tragedy of a drinking, psychotic wife who had deserted him and their five children 13 years ago and then reappeared for a few days in the neighborhood only last year, "like a ghost." Two of his three girls were grown now. The youngest was graduating from high school this year, and the oldest would be marrying a well-to-do young man in the summer. Mr. Kelly was especially proud of these two daughters and attributed their successes to the Catholic sisters who had reared them in a children's home for a number of years. The middle girl in her late teens, however, had dropped out of school, had little direction, and was starting to drink too much.

Darrell, now 16, had somehow always reminded Mr. Kelly of his wife and was often berated and harangued by his father. A slow learner in school, he had enjoyed the excitement and income he made from selling and using marijuana, and then speed. Darrell had had a brief psychotic break, spending several months in a psychiatric facility. He had also entered a drug treatment program and later moved to a residential child placement facility. Though Darrell was doing better now, Mr. Kelly did not want him to return home other than for an occasional weekend visit.

By contrast, 13-year-old Danny was the real joy of his life, even though he, too, was completely beyond Mr. Kelly's control. Danny was also starting to sell marijuana, just as his brother had, and he would stay out until all hours of the morning. Mr. Kelly had enrolled Danny in five different schools over the last two years, but Danny truanted each of them within a few days of the new enrollment. Each time Mr. Kelly threw up his hands, helplessly asking why.

In my first visit with Mr. Kelly, he poured out his life story in a chaotic jumble of anxious episodes. Excitedly, he said that he, Danny, and two of the girls now living with him would be forced to move again very soon—their twelfth move in the neighborhood in 13 years! The landlord was after him for back rent.

Moving away from landlords had become a way of life. Mr. Kelly collected welfare and said he was never sure if he would scrape together the next month's rent. He said he had not worked since his wife left. Transferring Danny to one more school, placing Darrell or the girls in various centers, or moving from apartment to apartment had become a full-time job. In his amiable way, he had stumbled and fumbled his way through these troublesome years.

As Mr. Kelly juggled before me the multiple crises of his life, expressing his bewilderments, his past and imminent dilemmas, it was also clear how much he thrived on the very events he so lamented. Now he was certain there was no other alternative for Danny than to go into placement. Good-humoredly and supportively, I noted that he had actually had a lot of excitement from his life. Sympathetically, I asked how would one get along without such ups and downs?

Mr. Kelly had clearly expected his new worker to try to hold him off in this latest placement request, as the former social workers had, whom he also, at times, so adroitly avoided. Instead, I suggested that we think of Danny's situation as requiring special preparation, for example, as if getting ready for a "fire drill." Although it would have made little sense to a more reasonable client, Mr. Kelly liked the analogy. Indeed, life was like going from one burning building to the next. Could one actually prepare oneself for the next fire? I suggested that in three days he march with Danny down to my office sharply at 9:30 A.M. We would not place Danny immediately, but rather go through a "dry run," as one goes through a drill in preparation for an emergency. I would discuss all the latest procedures for placement with him and with Danny and prepare them for this imminent crisis. I would not try to talk him out of it. A little baffled and confused, Mr. Kelly assured me he would be there.

In the office visit, for which he was 30 minutes early, I showed Mr. Kelly and Danny the routine placement forms and discussed the spectrum of placement choices—from the "ratty" drop-in centers to the "top-of-the-line" residential settings which were comparable to some boarding schools. Which did he want for his son? What would any caring father want? I explained that if he chose the "better placement" there would be a 2- to 3-month waiting period, and he would then have to prepare Danny for such an important move. These nicer places would certainly not want a kid who was selling drugs or truanting school! We would have to show them that this boy at least had enough motivation to improve in these two areas. Danny acknowledged that he didn't want to go to any of them; but if required to make a choice, he would prefer the better ones. I responded that he would then have to work with his father in order to earn his way there. The first step would be reentering and staying in school during the time the application was processed.

A few days after the office visit, Danny was unexpectedly picked up by the police on an old bench warrant and taken into delinquent court. In the court session, Mr. Kelly tried to impress an unsympathetic judge with his tales of woe. The judge was, however, quite provoked at Mr. Kelly's uncooperative history and was ready to place Danny immediately in a juvenile detention center. Stirred by the court battle and the probability of his son's removal, Mr. Kelly asserted (as I also coached him to do) that he was now working with the new family-oriented program. He promised the judge that he would re-enroll Danny in school and supervise him closely to assure that there would be no more delinquent violations. At this point, the judge agreed to return Danny to his father with a review of the case in 10 weeks.

Mr. Kelly was pleased that he had "beat the case" and he did not grasp that his real work had just begun until I arrived on his doorstep the day after the court hearing, reminding him of our scheduled conference with the school counselor! During this meeting, Danny sat silently. An agreement was reached among the adults. The father would check daily to determine that Danny had arrived at school, as Danny, under the pressure of the court, had also now agreed to attend. If Danny were *not* present, both the father and I would be called by the school counselor. Although Danny, "a tough kid," had remained impassive during the previous day's court hearing, he now buried his head in his hands during this meeting and cried softly. Had three adults ever really jointly agreed on anything affecting him before?

On the next day, however, Danny was not at school, nor had Mr. Kelly called the school. I realized it was not yet realistic to expect Danny to report to school on his own. Thus, on the third day, and for four consecutive days, I arrived at Mr. Kelly's door at 8:00 A.M. to support and challenge Mr. Kelly's enforcement of the service plan and court agreement with his son. Reluctantly, Mr. Kelly agreed with me that there was no other way to require Danny to attend school than to physically accompany him for a while. Resistant and embarrassed, Danny tried twice to break away from his father. "Stick with him," I urged the father, as we all trooped to school.

After taking him to his new classroom, Mr. Kelly blocked the classroom door as Danny made a single attempt to dart out. Tired and bewildered, Mr. Kelly asked what else he should do if the boy were going to run. I helped the father find a chair and advised him, with the teacher's consent, to sit outside the classroom door for the morning. Indeed, four mornings of accompaniment to school and sitting outside the classroom were required before the father understood his new role and Danny could internalize his father's intent: No more truanting would be allowed!

At this point Danny began to attend school on his own and within a few weeks to even achieve progress in the classroom. At the next court hearing, Mr. Kelly produced a note from Danny's teacher indicating that Danny had done so well in her class that he would be advanced two grades, that is, to his correct level, if he completed this school year. Danny and his father had allied to beat the delinqency system's earlier threat. Mr. Kelly then enjoyed complete victory before a rather baffled judge and became the talk of his neighborhood. They had accomplished with the support of the service team what had seemed impossible before.

"Danny back in school, after two years?" his sisters asked in astonishment, "Will it last?" Danny indeed completed the year and was successfully advanced. He had found that he had a father after all and he continued in school, distinguishing himself playing football during the next year. Perhaps almost without noticing it, as his father now felt capable of managing him at home, Danny, the last of the five children, had lost his turn at entering placement.

Chapter 6

PARENT–SCHOOL–CHILD TRIADS
Systemic Interventions

This chapter discusses the nuts and bolts of intervention into the parent–school–child system. How one gains entry into the system depends upon the nature of that system and the types of liaison activity that are feasible. The passively or aggressively entangled parent and school personnel are then prepared for a carefully orchestrated parent–school conference which opens effective communication and problem solving on behalf of the child.

GAINING ENTRY INTO THE SITUATION

Certainly the first and most preferable means of contact is through the client's direct initiative for services or through the client's self-referral based upon the school's recommendation for treatment. Such a case, as Aponte (1976) has illustrated in his discussion of an ecostructural school conference,[1] provides a basis for the social service agency or clinic to establish communication with the school. The therapist will call the school directly to arrange a meeting with relevant school personnel, the parents and child.

In view of the three types of triadic interactional systems, as discussed in Chapter 4, however, one would expect the parents in the passive or aggressive entanglement modes to be less likely to initiate their own referral or to follow up on school recommendations, as it is not in the nature of such rigidly closed systems to reach out by direct or voluntary means for assistance. Rather, such systems are more often characterized by an inability to seek change. They are indeed stalemated or locked, as we have seen, into repetitive cycles which escalate in intensity during crisis points but do not change in character by their own accord. In short, the self-referral is more likely to originate from the adaptive triadic system, i.e., from the parents who have not given up all hope in the schools or in the possibility of finding viable solutions.

Since the more stalemated aggressive or passive triadic systems are more likely to simply encourage the youth to drop out of school, the family service or child welfare agency must look for specific and active means to gain entry into these seemingly deadlocked situations. Privately funded or public agency programs which have access to juvenile referrals from the police department create an opportunity for direct intervention. These police referrals identify youth who have been picked up for truancy or for more severe acting-out behaviors, such as damaging school property or attacking another pupil or a teacher. Progressive police departments often welcome competent social service intervention as an alternative to lengthy court procedures or to the costly detention of youths with repeated offenses.

Another potential means of entry into the rigid system may be created by an agency which develops a collaborative relationship with a school district's official home and school visitor's office. Frequently, such offices are understaffed but are quite willing to work with counselors and professional social workers in the community who, with the legal presence of the home and school (attendance) office, can engage the parents and children. Such collaborative work has a coupling effect which increases the scope of client services when the school district office is limited in numbers of staff.

Thirdly, the social service organization concerned about the problematic interface of the family and school systems may choose to establish contact in local schools directly. Although the agency's program developer may talk directly to school personnel, he/she may gain access also through volunteer organizations—for example, by presenting a community education workshop to the parent–teacher's association or a similar group. Through such outreach efforts, interested teachers, administrators, or parent leaders within the generally problematic setting will begin to refer the more difficult cases in which they believe the active family service intervention can be useful.

Within such an agency program a specific individual(s) would be identified to work with particular schools. This designated school liaison would be the informed agency representative on matters of school procedure, discipline codes of the school, and due process rights of parents and children in relation to discipline issues.

In summary, the school liaison program would target the harder-to-reach clients where active outreach would be required. Steps for setting up the program would include:

1. Individual or group meetings with key personnel in the local schools (e.g., principal, vice-principal, counselors, and disciplinarians) to inform them of the agency's services and family-oriented service.
2. Presentation of positive examples of collaborative efforts, e.g., how parents with social service supports learn to work with school personnel to resolve issues.
3. Description of conferences set up by agency for parent and school personnel to hear everyone's input into problems and solutions and to establish new working relationships among the parent, school, and child.
4. Clarification of follow-up procedures including completion of reports to the school, and courts, when necessary.

Establishing Rapport with the Family

After contact is made between the social worker or other trained professional, e.g., therapist, and a family whose child is having difficulty (usually through a cordial letter offering a home visit at a particular time), the social worker will, as a part of his or her general assessment process, find it helpful to determine the typical response pattern of the parents to the school system. How do the parents react to various school professionals (for example, withdrawal or aggression)? Are the parents able to describe the problem from more than one perspective or are they locked into a very one-sided view? Do the parents align unconditionally with the child—either covertly or overtly? Do the parents' attitudes indicate hopelessness and helplessness? Are the parents immobilized by anger or depression?

As the social worker gains a clearer concept of the triadic interactional style of the parent, the school personnel, and the child, he/she will also develop rapport and a strategy for working with the particular type of system. With more aggressive or volatile parents, the professional will encourage the clients to ventilate their hostile feelings about the school to him/her, rather than at the already defensive or punitive school. The social worker will help the parents acknowledge the futility of continued hostile behaviors. Can the parents recognize how the child may be further labeled or victimized by such efforts? What new behaviors would the parents be willing to consider, with the support of the social worker, which would prevent the child's further decline in the school setting? What are specific ways in which the parents can begin to take charge of the child's behavior at home, if necessary? What are the objective needs of the child and how can they be articulated by the parents in ways that do not directly blame and accuse the school?

In a similar way, the professional prepares passively entangled parents for effective and collaborative communication with the school. With these clients, however, special attention is given to motivating them toward being more active and assertive. Are the parents aware of their parental and procedural rights—for example, reasonable notification of suspensions and unexcused absences, the right to review school records, and the right to appeal administrative decisions? Have the parents always gone to the school alone and would they want to make new efforts, in this case accompanied by the social worker who would help to facilitate communication? Have the parents ever had any positive experiences with any of their children's teachers? If so, what favorable points can be drawn from these experiences to enhance self-esteem and the parents' sense of personal strength and hope?

With both groups of parents, potential adaptive capacities or experiences should be recognized and encouraged. A particularly helpful means of promoting these dynamics is role playing. Using a role play enables the parents to practice more adaptive behaviors which the social worker can model for them. In this manner, the parents learn to articulate the child's needs in assertive but nonthreatening ways with school personnel. The parents are also encouraged to brainstorm some possible solutions with the social worker which may be negotiated, when appropriate, at the actual school conference.

SETTING UP THE FAMILY–SCHOOL CONFERENCE

The school should be notified as soon as possible regarding the genuine efforts of the family in working with the social worker toward resolving troublesome issues. Several weeks of work with the family will usually precede the school contact. With this knowledge the school is generally more willing to consider a meeting with the family. If there is initial resistance on the part of the school, for example, where the agency has not established a working relationship with the school, a pre-meeting between the social worker and the school counselor or vice principal is important. At this time, the social worker can explain the casework, the conference process and goals, and the social worker's primary role in facilitating this joint meeting. The pre-meeting sets the stage for the new and more productive dialogue between the family and the school.

The persons invited to the school conference itself are the relevant school personnel—principal or vice-principal, school counselor, and one or two teachers who know the child well. The invitation is usually through the school counselor, acting as the social worker's liaison within the school structure. The

family participants include the parents, the child and, sometimes, other siblings who may attend that same school.

The general format of the family–school conference opens
with an introduction by the social worker of the participants
and a positive statement of the purpose and goal for the
meeting. The goals of the meeting are twofold—to promote
constructive interaction and dialogue between the parents and
the school personnel, and to establish a working agreement
between the parties that will address the school-related
problem in a new and more cooperative manner. For example,
the teachers may agree to advise the parents on how to tutor
the child in a difficult subject area, with the parents and teachers checking in with each other for a specific number of weeks.
If testing has not been done, there may be an agreement to
conduct a comprehensive academic and psychological assessment, with a follow-up meeting to discuss the child's particular
educational needs.

If there have been attendance or behavioral problems on
the part of the youth, the parents and the teachers need to
agree upon a means to inform the parents regularly of progress or setback at school. Parents must also indicate how they
will reenforce the agreed-upon standards. The youth as well
expresses, whenever willing to do so, his or her needs, concerns, and feelings about school expectations, peer relations, or
academic or social issues; these stated needs are recognized as
much as possible in the development of solutions. For instance,
tutoring services may be needed, or the youth may need an
after-school job or recreational opportunity.

Above all, the beginnings of a clear and open working alliance are established in the presence of the child between the
parents and school personnel—a relationship that provides appropriate guidance and nurturance to the child about school
and educational issues.

OTHER CONSIDERATIONS

Some other general guidelines that would apply to systemic intervention include the following:

1. It is important for the school liaison or social worker to be quite well informed on school policy and due process rights of children and parents. Local school or district level hearings regarding a child's suspension or involuntary transfers (disciplinary or lateral), or special education entitlements, may be used as natural entry points for problem solving. While it is always preferable to have a family–school conference first, the case may not come to the attention of the agency until proceedings are initiated or more advanced. Efforts should be made by the agency professional to influence punitive tendencies toward constructive alternatives which address needs.

2. Also when the social worker assists the family in exercising due process rights, e.g., the right to inspect the child's official school records, the right to require hearings that contest administrative decisions, etc., it is advisable to seek to defuse adversarial qualities as much as possible. Language and professional skills will set a conciliatory tone. Consider, for example, the contrastive tones of the two statements, and the effects of each approach:

> It is the parent's right to review all records in absolute privacy!
>
> versus
>
> The parent and I would like to understand the child better and will be stopping by the school office at a convenient time next week to look over his records. . . . We look forward to meeting you . . . and are interested in your concerns about this child as well.

3. In general, it is best for the liaison or social worker to present themselves to all parties as go-betweens or mediators, e.g., helping to facilitate dialogue among the parties, appreciating publicly the concerns and needs of the parent *and* of the school, and providing support to the parent and child without being one-sided.

4. Where inappropriate suspensions, as for lateness, truancy, class cutting, or ID loss are occurring, the parent and social worker would seek as a minimum agreement that the school first notify the parent directly of any future student infractions. School officials will usually agree to this point when pressed by the parents to do so. Also, it is advisable to bring the

child back the first day of a suspension, rather than to wait the 3 to 5 days that may be indicated on the notification. If a parent presents the child early and insists that he/she be readmitted, the school will usually accept the child back early, with less class time lost.

A System That Works

The triadic assessment and intervention approaches described here are developed out of the social worker's awareness of the powerful influences that impact upon children and youth in the two essential contexts in which they live. Where there is a severe, unresolved conflict, overt or covert in nature, particularly between the values and expectations of the adults of the two systems, a stalemate often occurs, leading to the eventual dismissal of the child from the school setting or the child's dropping out. If the school system itself is unable to resolve the problem, the social worker's mediation effort with both systems can inspire the entangled parties to consider the possibility of new and mutual approaches that are less blaming and specific to the needs of the child. The social worker's active intervention relieves the pupil from the damaging triangulated position, making it possible for him/her to relate more appropriately and productively in the educational environment.

Chapter 7

LOCKED DOORS
A Vignette

Six-year-old Ralph spent his first five years in a highly abusive climate with his mother, who was a prostitute and herself the product of severe family violence and early childhood sexual abuse. Even as she demonstrated that she was beyond the constraints or direct help of the family service program, and would eventually be incarcerated, she introduced the team to her three-year-old son Daron's father, agreeing to entrust both boys to his care. An intensive in-home service was provided to this father and two young boys. The following vignette depicts Ralph's early months in public school—an enormous transition which dramatically tests Ralph's potential for adjustment in either the mainstream or special-education setting. The stepfather's relationship with a nurturant, though stressed, school personnel is actively facilitated by the family-oriented social worker, as is the child's new relationship to his stepfather and to the school. The vignette is written in some sections from the boy's point of view.

Today Ralph, aged six, had almost had a good day at school. He had hit no one and was relatively friendly with the other children on the playground. He had not thrown his milk at lunchtime, nor spit at the lunchroom aide.

When he went back to his classroom before afternoon recess to pick up his jacket and found the door locked, however, an infantile rage broke upon him like a sudden storm. By his

57

teacher Ms. Smith's report, it was a far more severe tantrum than any of the others he had had in his first three months of first grade.

"You fucking bitch," he screamed at her. "Make that goddamn door open. You're not going to put your fucking hands on my jacket. I hate this stupid school. You're no fucking good, fucking stealers!" Ralph's torrent of curses filled the hallways outside his classroom as he kicked the locked door that separated him from his jacket. If he had had a brick, he would have smashed the widowpane out of the door.

Ralph had been shut out by locked doors too many times before. Often he played on the stump of the steps outside his run-down house as his mother or aunt yelled at him from behind the locked front door to stay out of the "fucking house" until they were ready to let him in. It was not unusual for him to be forced to stay outside for hours. Sometimes he urinated on himself when they would not open the door.

Ralph didn't understand why his mother locked him out this way. Why did those men get to go in when they knocked nicely and said dumb things to his mother. One time he heard a man ask for "a piece of ass." Ralph knew that seemed to be the ticket for big people. Whenever he knocked and asked for it, though, it just made them laugh. Ralph knew that when he was older, he'd have a password that would work; then he would get in that door.

Once, just once, when he was four, Ralph had tried to knock down the door of the house, as he bashed it with a chunk of concrete from the litter on the sidewalk. He remembered how the concrete marked the outside of the door like chalk. If his mother Tracey didn't open that goddamn door, he would knock it off its hinges. It already wobbled a little bit, didn't it? How he wished to just smash it.

When his mother finally opened the door, yelling at him, she stood there like some statue made bigger than real people. "Get yourself in here, you little fucking bastard." She yanked him in, grabbing the shoulder of his dirty T-shirt so hard the ribbing burned his neck, and he shouted "Ow!"

"Get up to your fucking room, you little bastard," she screamed. "Didn't you hear me, you little tramp. Why did I ever have to have you anyway? You get up there now!"

Ralph couldn't move. He wanted to get up the steps, but he stayed stuck as if his shoes were glued.

His mother had screamed at other times and she had beaten him before, but today was different. She swayed more, and the look in her eyes was like fire. He looked back at her as if he couldn't take his eyes away.

But his looking at her seemed to make her even madder, as if he reminded her of somebody. People always said to her, "That boy's got all your looks, your eyes, and narrow shaped head and nose, and your slender build." They said it all the time.

"Why did *you* have to come into my life, you little bastard?" she screamed. "I should have flushed you down the fucking toilet. You're a devil to try to bust my door down. You're ruining my fucking life. You're going to get it this time, so you'll never forget it. Do you hear me?"

Those were the words. If she said anything else, he couldn't remember it later. He knew she picked up a broom with a thick handle. She hit his face and then on the back of his skinny shoulders and his legs. His bones seemed to be breaking. He heard his own voice screaming like it was somebody else's voice. When he finally did hear another person's voice he didn't know it at first. The voice screamed, "You want to kill that child? You want the neighbors calling the police?" Then his Aunt Peachie had hold of him and his mother was out the door.

Peachie washed the cut under his right eye. She checked his arms and legs. "Nothing's broken yet," she said. "Good thing I got here when I did." Ralph told her, "I'm just a bad kid. I'm even a devil."

Peachie bathed him, and even though it was only afternoon, put him to bed. She said he could go to sleep without worrying.

When his mother did finally come back, he stayed out of her way. In fact he could hardly make himself look at her. Tracey asked how was he doing, but he knew she didn't like him. She did seem to like his little brother Daron, who wasn't even three years old yet. Tracey would put Daron on her lap and fuss over him, even take him out with her sometimes. She would be gone for a couple of hours, and Daron would come back wearing new sneakers or a new shirt. Ralph didn't say anything. He thought if he stayed quiet enough, maybe she would start to like him. At least, he thought, she wouldn't hurt him.

Today had almost been a good day at school. He hadn't hit anyone. He hadn't spit at anyone. He hadn't thrown his milk at lunchtime—but they should not have locked his good jacket in the room behind the door. Especially not today, his last day at the school. He knew they were going to keep it.

The teacher took him into the counselor's office. He knew the office well. That's where he had gone many times before. He stayed there a long time, until his stepdad Bill arrived.

Ralph and Daron had been away from their mother for months now. For a few weeks they stayed with a foster mother, Ms. Green, the lady with the nice house. Then Daron's father (who was Ralph's stepfather) started to visit them and told the social worker that he would like to have both of them live with him and their grandmother.

Ralph liked Daron's father and called him Daddy from the first day they moved into his house. Even though Bill would sometimes shout at him and spank him, and even though Bill sometimes drank too much and came home very late, Ralph idealized him. Ralph trusted him because he knew how he too hated his mother. It only really hurt Ralph when Bill sometimes said he looked and acted like her.

Today he was afraid his new father would be mad at him for having to come from work for a meeting at school. The social worker was at the meeting too. It must be a big deal for all these people to be here.

Ralph wasn't so sure how he felt about Ms. Smith. She shouldn't be making him leave this school. Sometimes he had called her a "fat fucking bitch" when he was really mad. She *was* fat. He had never seen anyone so big. And he didn't want her to know that leaving the school mattered. "What a stupid school!" he kept saying.

She had locked his jacket in the room. He could not believe it was just a mistake; he was sure she was acting like his mom. The fat bitch was going to keep it, he thought.

At the school meeting, his new father's sister showed up also. She had a special way of talking with him as she asked him about the door and the jacket and what had made him so very angry. He said he just wanted the jacket. It was *his*.

Then the social worker wanted to know if he could say why he was leaving this school. Ralph looked back at him and answered softly, "Because I'm bad."

"No," replied the worker. "I thought you might say that. Ms. Smith, can you tell Ralph why he will be leaving this school today?"

Ms. Smith spoke gently. "Ralph, you're not leaving the school because you're bad. You're a good person, and I like you very much. Remember, I told you I would like to spend more time with you, but there are too many kids in the class-room. You have so many questions all the time. With thirty kids, I can't always answer you and help you enough. You're going to be going to a school where there will be only six or seven children in your classroom. Your new teacher will be able to help you much more often. I know sometimes you've done some wrong things, but I like *you*, Ralph, and I'm going to miss you."

Then Ms. Smith took him to his classroom to pick up his jacket and other things, and to to say good-bye to his friends. Although he was leaving the school today, he was not being locked out. It wasn't like that after all.

Chapter 8

THE CROSS-CULTURAL DANCE OF
THE PROFESSIONAL AND CLIENT

From the social change and liberation movements of the past 25 years in the United States, an extensive body of literature addressing cultural or ethnic-sensitive social service practice has emerged. Whether the social service is directed toward black families,[1-3] Puerto Ricans,[4-6] Polish immigrants,[7] Korean and Japanese war brides,[8] or Navojos of Utah,[9] the social worker's appreciation of the client group's distinctive cultural patterns, native language, ethnic values, and familial and community behaviors is critical. A significant theme is the inherent differences in the family among the various groups, e.g., the supportive kinship network which has, in the midst of poverty and great oppression, historically promoted survival for many black families,[1] the special supportive function of the black church,[10] the roles of the *compadres, padrinos,* and *hijos de crianza* in the augmented Puerto Rican family,[5] or the matrifocal elements of the Navajo family.[9]

In addition to the anthropological and cultural characteristics, the sociological perspective outlines many points of stress in social functioning and adjustment for the minority client within a dominant culture which demands conformity. Certainly major discord occurs as the majority culture imposes its values of competition, individualism, and productivity upon cultures which, by and large, are more socially and expressively oriented. Dissonance is most evident for the individual or family where it relates to the other necessary systems of the society, e.g., schools, jobs, housing, and social services,[5] which are usually controlled by the majority culture.

The matter of providing effective social and educational services to minority clients is complicated, however, by well-intentioned professionals, who may seek solutions to the adjustment difficulties of their clients—but from a majority viewpoint that excludes the full and respectful participation of those parties who are to be served. Such misguided, uninformed helpfulness is poignantly described by B. Montalvo in his discussion of home–school conflicts involving Puerto Rican children:

> Good intentions are manifested by teachers with a bilingual approach, by reaching-out teachers, and by programs for parent involvement, by alert and humane counselors, and by outside clinicians. Yet the youngsters' situations seldom change. Many continue to be placed in conflict regarding their language, appearance, relationship style, or aspirations. (Ref. 11, p. 101)

Spurred by more culturally appropriate professionals, a number of common principles of practice and ethnic-sensitive services models[1,12,13] have been created. Central to many of these approaches is the principle of "following the demand of the client task," in contrast to the professional's redefining of the needs of clients in specialized terms. Devore and Schlesinger summarize their basic working assumptions as follows:

1. Individual and collective history have bearing on problem generation and solution.
2. The present is most important.
3. Nonconscious phenomena affect individual functioning.
4. Ethnicity is a source of cohesion, identity, and strength as well as a source of strain, discordance, and strife. (Ref. 12, p. 134)

These approaches are broad-based, recommending intervention with both the individual at the casework level and with larger social systems at the policy and program levels. While tension has existed for years between these two practice areas, ethnic-sensitive casework that promotes the development of the individual client or family may also provide an informed foundation for advocacy to change oppressive organizational or societal structures.

Perhaps the best resolution of this inherent tension is found in systems theory, which seeks to explain patterns of process and organization that contribute to the larger social gestalt(s). The systems approach provides a broader and more integrative analysis of the ethnicity dilemma, as it widens the assessment of problems from the individual or family to the patterns of transactions of the client with the systems of the neighborhood and larger society. The Black Task Force Report of the Family Service Association of America is an example of this more expansive outlook, as commented on by W. Green:

> This perspective does not negate a psychodynamic approach but broadens the area of concern to structural factors which impinge on the lives of black persons and which may be determining influences of the problems that first brought the individual or family to the attention of the social agency. (see Ref. 10, p. 98)

Thus, according to the systems view, society develops dominant hierarchies from which sophisticated, intricate (usually unconscious) patterns of behavior occur among the interdependent entities that comprise the social structure and that perform the functions of the society. The oppressiveness of this complex social system in a biased dominant culture is aptly stated by Schermerhorn:

> Yet they (dominant group) cannot press their advantage too far without raising serious opposition, trouble, and disorder from those in lower echelons. Even in order to exploit them, the privileged must see to it that those in subordinate positions not only subsist, but are motivated to continue playing their roles in a system to which both upper and lower groups contribute, though in functionally different ways . . . the upper stratum finds itself driven to accept responsibility for satisfying minimal requirements of those in lower status positions and motivating them to continue their necessary activities. (see Ref. 10, p. 98)

Akin to the systems view is the bicultural or dual perspective (Norton et al.). From the nurturing and intimate system of the family the individual develops a sense of identity and knows "oneself through role taking and from the reflections of others."[15] As this self interacts with the larger social systems, called the "sustaining system," harsh dissonances will often occur for the minority individual or family, when the dominant society wittingly or unwittingly violates the dignity and self-worth of others different from itself. An attitudinal and cognitive tool, the dual perspective juxtaposes the various elements of the complex subsystems in which the minority individual or family lives, focusing on the degree of incongruence, particularly between the family and the larger society or sustaining system. The purpose of the dual perspective is to promote "understanding and sensitivity to the totality of the life situation of the (minority) client group and to build services on the needs of that particular situation" (see Ref. 15, p. 3).

THE CROSS-CULTURAL DANCES: INTRODUCTION

Having reviewed basic themes in the cross-cultural social service literature, my further purpose in this chapter is to describe within the social service—education—family settings several primary cross-cultural styles and sequences of behaviors. These common patterns of interaction which are varieties of cross-cultural dance(s) occur in the context of providing services, when the client and the professional are of different ethnic origins. The dance(s) of assimilation are based upon the styles of conflict of the social worker and the client family. The second set of transactions, the adaptive cross-cultural dance, however, reflects a willingness of the two parties to gradually develop trust and to establish a working relationship in which there is mutual respect for cultural difference.

Finally, the optimal social service modality, which for purposes of our discussion will be called the cross-cultural or syntonic team approach, models for the client effective cross-cultural relationships among a small personalized team of service providers. This cross-cultural relationship is accessible to the client, especially through at least one team member of the same ethnic origin, and extends the experience of the client and worker alike. In particular, the bicultural dissonances between the client's family and the dominant culture may be more readily addressed.

While the interactive process between the service provider and ethnically different client reflects the essential elements of intersystemic human interaction and styles of conflict and adaptation, the context is much more highly charged than that of social interaction with clients of the same background. Indeed, there is greater probability for misunderstanding, whether through ignorance of the other's language, verbal and behavioral miscues, false assumptions of sameness or difference, or lack of awareness of cultural values, habits, and behaviors. Further turbulence in the professional and client cross-cultural relationships may result from either inappropriate behaviors of the professional or from unresolved pain of the minority client whose old hurts may be restimulated. Such restimulation can occur when the client is reminded by a current interaction, (whether it is an inappropriate one or not), of a previous uncomfortable or unresolved behavioral event.

THE DANCES OF ASSIMILATION

One of the more common of the cross-cultural dances evident in educational and social service settings is the dance of assimilation, and it appears in a variety of intricate transactional forms. While overtly biased behavior of a service professional would usually be the subject of public censure, the more covert transactional style of oppression—often an unconscious process—is more prevalent, more elusive, and thus more difficult to confront. Montalvo[11] provides a number of illustrations of well-meaning professionals in many settings, who, while espousing open views of other cultures, unwittingly demonstrate ignorance about the new culture, a fear and suspicion of difference, or behaviors of excessive control. An underlying arrogance prevails in the professional posture which seeks to help the client of a different ethnic origin—but clearly and exclusively in the helper's terms. The result of the more subtle underlying behavior which is depicted, for instance, in the case of a school sponsoring an experimental cross-cultural program,[11] but treating the Hispanic parent aide as a maid, is a statement of bias and conformity to the social order. Indeed, the ambivalence of such a transaction provokes uneasiness, confusion, and hostility in many forms.

The response of the client to such pressured assimilative cultural behavior, whether subtle or overt within the service or educational contexts, may be of several transactional varieties. A passive dance of assimilation occurs when there is an acquiescence to oppressive behavior by the ethnically different client, either because of feelings of intimidation, or lack of knowledge about viable alternatives. In the social–family context the overt compliance may result in the parent pushing the child to conform or to assimilate to the cultural expectations of the school, while also being very angry at the school or child. The minority child is then in a double bind, since adherence to the dominant culture's overt message of conformity and compliance places the obedient child at the risk of being also disloyal to the family, particularly if its affective signals contradict spoken parental directives.

A second variation of the transaction may be called the aggressive dance of assimilation. Here again the professional operates with a covert message of social conformity, despite more obvious appearances of providing legitimate services or an education experience. A hostile, aggressive response to the professional, in this instance by the parent, will push the school to either side more strongly with the child against the parent (a position which the child would find untenable) or the school may subject the child to further harassment. Either reaction of triangulation by the school or family may predispose the child to act out in peculiar ways or to simply disengage from the painful cultural dissonance by dropping out of school altogether.

While these systemic dances reflect the styles of triangulated conflict described in Chapter 4, such problems within the cross-cultural context, because it is more highly charged, will require the skillful intervention of a facilitator who can operate from the dual cultural perspective. Appropriate joint intervention into both culturally different systems is usually necessary in a case-specific manner.

THE ADAPTIVE CROSS-CULTURAL DANCE

Even when the professional is cognizant of systemic operations and maintains a sophisticated dual cultural perspective, transactions between the worker and client of different ethnic backgrounds will be charged at certain points with dynamic tension. Indeed, one can anticipate misunderstandings to arise at times which challenge the integrity of the relationship on either side. In discussing the vulnerability of such a relationship between a white professional and a lower-income black client, for example, Gitterman observes:

> In this encounter, as in society, it is the white professional who has the perceived and defined power, status, and control. This predefined, institutionalized role relationship triggers deep feelings of mistrust, anger, fear, pain, and resentment within both worker and client. These feelings represent potential obstacles to the development of a helping relationship through which desired services can be delivered. . . . Thus, those obstacles that impede the development of such a helping relationship must be dealt with by worker and client in order for them to work successfully. (Ref. 3, p. 291)

Therefore, the adaptive cross-cultural dance does not idealistically presume the absence of actual or potential conflict, but rather a readiness or at least willingness on the part of the two parties to address difficulties when they occur. This adaptive process is usually characterized by an initial phase of cautiousness or distancing, followed by a gradual development of trust. Intimacy achieved too readily may be interpreted as demonstrating a lack of respect for genuine cultural differences and setbacks may occur as a way to redistance the parties and slow the pace of the developing relationship. Racial and cultural misunderstanding as defensive processes may also protect the client or worker from other uncertainties, insecurity, and pain.

In the following case of the McGillis family, a white working-class family serviced in a child protective agency by a black social worker, stages of development in the cross-cultural dance indicate periods of careful distancing, client manipulation and pressure, conflict, and reconciliation. The McGillis family came to the attention of the child protective agency after several reports of injuries to their very young children, which were not adequately explained as "accidents." The social worker sensed in the first stage a very polite distance on both her part and the client's as each "tried not to offend the other." A quite needy and dependent client, Ms. McGillis, however, then actively sought the engagement and direct assistance of the worker, thereby acquiring child-specific services, e.g., day care. Within a brief time, Ms. McGillis began to make rather extraordinary demands on the social worker's time, e.g., multiple calls to the worker on consecutive days. Although the worker was genuinely responsive to the client, she took responsibility for setting necessary limits on her time and for helping to pace the relationship. The client responded by applying excessive pressure, including notification of the attorney who had represented the parents in the child protective court action that she was not receiving enough services.

By her own acknowledgment, the worker tolerated such pressure at the beginning more patiently from this white family than she might have from a black family. However, as she began to feel exploited by Ms. McGillis and her husband, she realized that overt conflict would be inevitable. Prior to a routine court review of the case, the parents' attorney complained in the presence of the parents directly to the worker about the worker's lack of responsiveness to the client's expressed needs. Ready for this confrontation, the worker provided a list of extensive service accomplishments and asserted that if the clients' were not satisfied with her work or who she was, they could certainly request a replacement.

The worker's professional indignation caught the family (and attorney) by surprise, and both spouses, realizing the ded-

ication of the worker, became apologetic and respectful in a
new way. The black worker who had been polite and nurturant
also appropriately refused to be demeaned. Her challenge to
the parents and the attorney was based upon her own self-
respect as well as her genuine concern for the client. Fortu-
nately, this occasion provided the bridge to a stronger and
more honest working relationship.

Therefore, while the dualistic cross-cultural working relationship is possible in many forms, its considerable risks are
also apparent. Reconciliation, for example, may not occur.
Or, the necessary give-and-take required in the formation of a
difficult cross-cultural relationship may not be feasible, even
where the social worker is truly ethnicically sensitive. In short,
the development of trust may be long and exacting for either
party and it may delay the immediate usefulness of the service.

Further, when the relationship is not essentially a voluntary one, as in child welfare, public education, or delinquency
services, the client may feel especially trapped and without
ready access to an understanding professional of the same ethnic origin. Racial and ethnic obstacles sometimes serve as an
overt or covert excuse for avoiding engagement and services
altogether.

For these reasons, the matching of social workers of the
same ethnic origin as the client has become a preferred service
delivery option for many agencies, at least when they have the
available minority personnel. This alternative, although of
great practical value in certain instances, may not be feasible,
nor, in this author's view, is it necessarily optimal, since the
matched client and social worker may operate within the limits
of their known cultural context and thereby avoid a cross-
cultural relationship altogether. Indeed, the beneficial experience of dealing with the cross-cultural tension which the client
may be encountering in their broader social–familial experiences may remain unaddressed.

THE CROSS-CULTURAL OR SYNTONIC TEAM APPROACH

In this writer's view, the cross-cultural or syntonic team
provides a modality for optimal service delivery. In order to be

culturally appropriate, the syntonic team will consist of at least
one member of the same ethnic group as the client. This individual helps to assure that the service takes into account the
values, customs, and language of the client. At the same time,
the team models for the client through its composition and behavior what a meaningful cross-cultural relationship is. This
working relationship of team members of different ethnic
backgrounds serves as both a practical bridge in the delivery of
services, for example, greater access of the team and client to
resources within the ethnic resource system, and as an example
of effective bicultural communication for the client. Clearly,
the demonstration of trust among the cross-cultural team will
more easily afford the building of trust between the client and
all of the team members. Team integrity, needless to say, requires the readiness of the small working group to acknowledge their own differences and to resolve them responsibly.

This cross-cultural or syntonic team, which is described in
more detail and from a treatment point of view in Chapter 10,
may be organized from personnel within the agency, from col-
laterals of other agencies, or from the client's own personal
community network. An interagency approach, for instance,
may include a white protective services worker and a black or
Hispanic therapist for a black or Puerto Rican family, respec-
tively. Use of the personal community might provide the inclusion of a mature and trusted neighbor, pastor, or teacher of
the client's ethnic origin in the small working team. The critical
issue here is that an assigned social worker of different ethnic
origin should make every effort to engage, for the sake of the
client, a collateral worker or other appropriate individual of
the same cultural background as the client—whom the client
may more readily trust.

CONCLUSION

This chapter has offered an overview of many of the major themes in the literature dealing with cross-cultural social
work. The transactional patterns that occur cross-culturally be-

tween families and social service and educational systems suggest that the cross-cultural dance of the professional and client
may occur in both problematic or in creative, adaptive forms.
The dance of assimilation, initiated by the pressures of the
dominant culture, may be acted out overtly or covertly through
client responses of hostile passivity or angry, more aggressive
entanglements. These transactions may be quite damaging
when either the family or the social institution permanently
withdraws without finding alternatives or resolutions to the
conflict, or when children or other family members are scapegoated in ongoing ambivalent and untenable triadic relationships among their family and the larger social service system.
An adaptive, dyadic cross-cultural dance was described, along
with its inherent risks. However, the optimal service delivery
modality appears to be one that models effective bicultural relationships among a small personalized team and which makes
accessible to the client the broader benefits of a meaningful
cross-cultural experience.

Chapter 9

COURTING FEAR
A Vignette

A client family's 10-year history of involvement with child protective services and the criminal justice system provides the backdrop for the courtroom vignette that follows. Responding to this older mother Marla's pleas for help with her out-of-control twin 15-year-old daughters and her own claims of victimization, professionals were usually led into scapegoating the father, thereby overlooking the mother's instigating role. The new family-oriented interagency approach includes for the first time many conjoint sessions with mother, her teenage daughters, and infant grandson. Separate contacts are made with the estranged father. These sessions are useful in bringing explosive incidents into perspective and in helping to defuse potentially dangerous situations. The biracial interagency team, consisting of a black family therapist and white child protective social worker, along with several staff members of a short-term placement center, maintain a high level of collaborative effort. Common goals are to establish appropriate behavioral outlets for anger for each member of the family, to enhance clearer verbal communication, to correct distortions promoted by various family members, and to help to relieve some measure of Marla's extreme stress and fear.

Marla, a 55-year-old mother and grandmother, walked in great haste from the courtroom after the review hearing. Furious, frightened, she was also nearly out of breath. The emotional wounds and controlling fears had been quite unexpectedly laid bare. This time she could not blame her 15-year-old twins Diane and Susan. Straightforward questions had required disclosures which were very uncomfortable for Marla. The mask had slipped for a moment.

Usually, Marla relished her court appearances. Few parents were better prepared to cite the failings of their children in society and at school. Chewing her words like a country preacher, Marla would testify fervently that she only wanted what was best for her girls. She insisted that they come home each night at a reasonable hour, attend school daily, and not bring men into the house. Weren't these the things that any self-respecting mother wants, Marla would ask rhetorically.

Unfortunately, however, neither Diane nor Susan attended school regularly. On the few occasions when Susan did go to the neighborhood high school, she was likely to be suspended for fighting. Diane had stopped attending completely. Both girls were sexually active with their boyfriends, Diane having already an 18-month-old son whom she called "Mopsie."

Six months ago, Marla contended before the judge, an alarming incident occurred. As she tried to take the phone away from Diane, an angry physical struggle ensued in which Diane allegedly drew a butcher knife and cut Marla's forehead. Though Marla had not seen the knife, the emergency room doctor, she said, told her it looked like a knife wound. On this basis, Diane was placed in a children's psychiatric hospital and later transferred into a residential placement setting.

Marla lamented that she had no control over the twins. Indeed, she knew they rode on the shoulders of their father, who lived only 12 blocks away and who hated her for the bitter 20 years of their former marriage. Besides, Marla had reported him to child protective services alleging that he had beaten Susan with a rubber hose. Now she believed he was trying to pay her back by turning the girls against her.

Diane continued to insist that she had used no knife in the earlier struggle. Her mother was simply imagining things, as usual. Perhaps the phone itself had hit her head, or there could have been a rough object on the sofa that she had stumbled onto.

It was always difficult to know who to believe in this explosive and accusatory family, where seldom a week passed when there was not at least one threatening shouting match on the street in front of their home. Neighbors had learned long ago to either close their doors or to call the police when the sound of the fights reached their highest pitch.

On the most desperate occasions, Marla sometimes spoke of "hiding all the knives." She seemed terrified and yet fascinated by the thought of violent clashes. Such imaginings could become real. She knew all too well that her son, Damiano, would continue to spend the better part of his life in prison for the fatal stabbing of another youth.

Thus, Marla again today presented herself in court as a mother who had suffered tragically in life. Her fearful distortions and projections continued to mask the many ways in which she subtly sabotaged efforts to resolve problems. While she publicly ordered the girls to attend school, she quietly refused to provide them with necessary money for public transportation to the school. Though she did not want them staying out late at night, she loaned them keys to return at any hour. Playing the ostensible role of a cooperative client, Marla frequently misconstrued information within the family, engendering confusion and rage.

Although being separated from her son during the week in the new placement setting, Diane had on weekends discovered genuine maternal affection for her son Mopsie which had not previously been so apparent. She clearly enjoyed tending him on her weekend visits at home, and she missed him during the week. In the family counseling sessions, Diane had made the most gains, as she learned to verbally express her anger in more appropriate or respectful ways and to identify her needs. She no longer used violence toward her family or peers. Diane's account of the original fight between her mother and herself remained consistent and became increasingly credible.

Marla, however, could not tolerate Diane's maturing behavior and increasing good judgment, nor would she accept any parental credit for Diane's progress. Change, whether positive or negative, was a terrifying process. What right did one of her last two children have to grow up and perhaps to move away from her for good? What deceptions and secrets might be revealed through all of these discussions? Above all else, Marla was quite jealous of the affection and nurturance Diane received in the residential placement center.

During a home visit, Diane played a game of peekaboo with Mopsie, skimming his light blue blanket over his face. His giggles and squeals of delight filled the room. Diane could not remember when she had enjoyed him so much. Observing this innocent behavior, Marla was overwhelmed by her worst fears and accused Diane of trying to kill her baby.

Incredulous, Diane sought out her counselor for support and direction. She felt she might never be able to trust her mother again, and prepared at this point to enter a teenage mother–infant shelter with Mopsie. But today's court testimony cracked the facade of Marla's deception. Her anxious machinations were becoming increasingly evident. Most startling to Marla at the hearing, however, was the social worker's clear assessment that Diane had certainly not endangered her infant. If Marla had indeed been a victim throughout her life, she was also the shrewd designer of much of the fearful chaos and violence that characterized her family.

Catching up with Marla as she waited at the bus stop on this chilly afternoon outside the courthouse, the worker sought to repair the unexpected wound which had been opened. "Marla, you know as I do that Diane did *not* try to kill her baby—perhaps you fear these things. I want you to be fair with your daughters, though. Yes, Diane is growing up. Perhaps you can tell me what is so very fearful for you."

Her guard down for just a moment, Marla looked with a puzzled expression at the social worker. A smile flickered quickly across her face as she stepped onto the bus which had just arrived. She wondered to herself if those things he said to her just might have some truth.

SYNTONIC TEAMS
A Psychodynamic/Systems Approach

A syntonic team, as the term is used here, is first of all family and community focused, and adapted as much as possible "to become resonant" with both the intrapsychic needs of the client and the systemic and concrete social needs of the client. This small personalized team may be developed by the clinical social worker or any other family service professional when the family's full range of needs exceeds what the individual helper is able to directly address. The adaptive syntonic team may consist, for instance, of a therapist, school counselor or probation officer, etc., working closely with the coordinating social worker. Where these professionals are from several agencies, the ongoing collaborative relationships also may be referred to as an "interagency team" (see also Chapter 14.) Additional team members as needed can also include mature individuals from the client's own kinship or social network.

This chapter is divided into two parts. The purpose of the first section is to provide a clinical foundation for syntonic teams. This theory illuminates the profound interactional/systems dimension of psychodynamic process, and develops out of both traditions. These theories, the psychoanalytic and systems views, in unison create a new whole greater than the sum of their parts, suggesting a range of deep emotional and structural needs of the client family. An assessment of these needs provides the basis for an adaptive team response.

The second section of the chapter describes the function, roles, and postures of the service and therapeutic team itself which develops after a broad assessment is made of the family within its community context. The professional who, for our purposes, is referred to as the social worker, but who could have a different title in other settings, assumes primary therapeutic and service responsibility, organizing, on an as-needed basis, a small, closely knit team which, over a period of time, becomes a new introject, or deep emotional frame of reference and source of support for the client family.

Part I: Core Concepts

The beginning of the twentieth century heralded the supremacy of the individual in almost all areas of western culture, including medicine, architecture, politics, and commerce. In the emerging field of psychology, Freud's writings provided dramatic and controversial insights into the workings of the individual human psyche. By mid-century, a number of "defectors," including Adler, Jung, and Rank, had challenged Freudian orthodoxy, particular around issues of symbolization. For example, the suprapersonal, nonsexual or symbolic elements of the oedipal complex, qualities having to do with family continuity and community, were considered more important than the literal sexual or incest taboo.[1] Nevertheless, the Freudian view continues to provide a substantial foundation,[2,3] giving rise to many new and extended psychoanalytic paradigms. Piaget provided an understanding of children's intellectual and cognitive development;[4] Erickson, a schema of lifelong developmental stages and goals[5]; and, more recently, Lifton, a paradigm based upon death and the continuity of life.[1] Concurrently, Mahler, Bowlby, and other object-relations theorists provided sophisticated and rich analyses of the earliest emotional and cognitive experiences of infants and young children which appear to form and mold personality,[6,7] growing out of interactional behaviors of the parent and child.

Also by the late 1950s and up to the present time, systems

theorists, in a spirit akin to intellectual revolution, have proclaimed a major paradigm shift from the individual psyche to the family system. Early studies of schizophrenia in the context of the family, including the double-bind theory,[8] ushered in a gamut of family therapy orientations, each seeking to clearly differentiate from the predominant psychoanalytic framework, at times subsuming it or even rejecting it.[9]

Some successful and very helpful efforts have been made in more recent years to show the comparative relationships of some of these family therapy schools, e.g., Minuchin, Olson, Wynne, and Bowen's notions of disengagement, differentiation, mutuality, and fusion as "separate-connectedness" characteristics of the family system.[10] Nevertheless, the gap between the psychodynamic and systems schools continues to be quite wide. Although psychosocial theorists suggest that a bridge between theories of psychoanalytic thought and systems thinking is possible, only selected illustrations have been presented thus far. For example, it is clear that the psychodynamics of internalization, introjection, or the trading of dissociations are reflected in current transactional contexts and reenactments, and that an understanding of personality theory could enhance the clinician's assessment of the current interactional system.[11] The powerful transferential therapeutic relationship as an active means for nurturing, disciplining, and programming the client, as described by D. A. and S. Kirschner, also breaks new ground in providing a theoretical synthesis, offering novel techniques for radically changing the family system.[12]

SYSTEMIC PSYCHOLOGICAL BIRTHING

Western culture's longstanding preoccupation with the individual self—indeed, in its most extreme form, the myth that the self can exist as a complete entity alone and unto itself—derives perhaps from the earliest feelings of omnipotence of the newborn infant. In these early weeks of life the new infant exists in a "dual unity," unable to perceive the separate existence of the other person upon whom it is totally dependent.[7]

From this still submerged identity, the mother and infant, as an intimate dyad, develop rhythms and patterns of mutual biological and emotional behaviors and responses attuned to the infant's needs and the mother's capacities. The quality of the bonding and of the ongoing maternal care gives form to the earliest transactions, making possible the gradual emergence of a distinctive individual self over the next few years.

The temperment of the baby itself, e.g., its relative degree of activeness or metabolic pace, along with the mother's range of feelings and skills also creates a myriad of interactional possibilities for this new human dyadic system. How well does the mother accept the fusion of the earliest phases? How comfortable is she with such powerful degrees of interdependency in which her own emotional and biological states (e.g., sleeping and nursing) are synchronized with the infant's? Will she scrutinize and accept her infant, bonding deeply and affectionately? Will she give regular eye contact and nurturant smiles to her new one? Is she able to understand and to validate the baby's patterned, practicing behaviors, or is she most often bothered or bewildered by its behaviors? Is the mother herself individuated enough to be able to rest and to restore herself while the baby sleeps or is occupied? Will she be threatened by or become overly anxious at her toddler's new and separate ventures into selfhood, its attempts to crawl, to walk away from her, or to assert its own discovery of self through the assertion of "No!"? Will the infant's natural separation anxieties reactivate unresolved anxieties in the mother? Will she smother the child with her concerns or allow it space to explore, but also to return to her as "home base"?

From the attachment–separation interplay her young child will ultimately achieve a rapprochement from which its separate identity will emerge. Through this interactional process the infant/toddler will either learn to enjoy exploration and learning or to experience shame, mistrust, and excessive fear. From intrapsychic, object-relations, or interactional frameworks, a harmony or balance of behaviors, mutual need fulfillments, and appropriate emotional states are sought between the mother and infant, which will enable the child to relate with confidence and curiosity toward its environment and the people in it.

Undergirding this dyadic process is the father, who may provide significant emotional support to the new pair; or if he is uncomfortable with the mother-infant attachment, he may in some form try to diminish or to interrupt it. How well will the spouses adapt their own relationship to recognize the needs of each other? Will the new triadic relationships include responsiveness of each one to the other? Will the couple identify and be able to delay (but not forget) the fulfillment of their own needs as the new infant and young child bursts forth with its claims?

The patterns of behavior which are established, e.g., who does what for whom and in what order, create a new homeostasis for the young family at this phase. How the family organizes itself, its ability to accept the separate parental and spousal intimacy of the dyads, its validation of the separate spheres or subsystems of emotional relationship, including the formation of a sibling subsystem, will greatly determine how well the child individuates, perceives, and relates to the world in general. The profound interactional and emotional imprints of the personality, especially one's deepest sense of self-esteem, confidence, and trust in self and others, arise out of these early concrete relational experiences of the family. Likewise, how well the mother and father themselves were psychologically birthed—that is, their own range of differentiation and degree of resolution of separation anxiety—will greatly influence their current capacities to understand, to nurture, and to guide their own young infant and child.

THE TRIADIC OR STRUCTURAL TEMPLATE

The much-sung oedipal phase, whether interpreted in orthodox or neo-Freudian ways, is also, upon closer scrutiny, a triadic interactional systemic struggle of great significance to the child and family. And it too in the early formative years, seems to imprint upon the child's mind and experience a fundamental configuration of authority and gender relationships, from which the individual, as a child and later as an adult, will interpret the world. Indeed, this period creates the weave of

the family's psychic and behavioral fabric, including the interactional dance, the structural boundaries, the roles of the same
and opposite sex parents, probable gender identification, and
ultimately the ethical or worldview (superego) of the child.

As the young child individuates, becoming more aware of
its own separateness or self, it may struggle to assert control
over the spousal subsystem—if it can. The little boy typically
asserts his wishes to grow up and "marry Mommy," as the
daughter looks forward to "marrying Daddy," thereby displacing the same-sex parent in fantasy and, at other times,
through actual behavioral struggles. A little boy may say that
he does not want his father to return from an out of town trip,
since he is now Mommy's little man of the house. Or a young
girl may be quite angry with her mother for interrupting her
story time with her dad to prepare her for bed.

Reasonably differentiated parents observe this phenomenon usually with some quiet amusement and acceptance. They
do not compete with the child, but remain securely in their
higher parental role. The same-sex parent gives continuing direction to the child, e.g., the mother completes daily tasks with
her daughter while also respecting the special warmth and
nurturance inherent in the child's relationship with her father.

The resolution of this triadic oedipal struggle occurs as the
child comes to understand the limits or boundaries of fundamental relationships, especially the roles of each parent. The
little boy learns that he cannot have the same intimate relationship with his mother that his father has. He cannot "conquer"
his father. With this realization he discovers respect for his father, and ultimately wishes to be like this influential, powerful,
unconquerable man.

Similarly, the daughter learns that she cannot conquer her
mother. Mother is too strong—indeed, nonplussed by the competition, having her own secure relationship with her husband.
The young daughter likewise learns to accept this boundary,
respecting her strong mother, with whom she can now more
deeply identify.

Thus, from this resolution of the triadic struggle, system
boundaries are made very clear to the child. The subsystem of
all of the children emerges as the appropriate location for peer

relationships, and the natural power and status of the parent is imprinted. Gender identification is enhanced from the respect which the child acquires for the "powerful" parent. Simultaneously, the opposite-sex parent continues to be experienced as the loving, nurturant parent, the parent who is able to intervene or to facilitate with the usually more authoritative same-sex parent. Though able to intervene on the child's behalf, the loyalty of the opposite-sex parent to her spouse remains undisputed.

In a profound manner, occurring both interactionally and emotionally, the child's experience is imprinted with relationship structures and deep meanings, including a sense of appropriate familial loyalties, an understanding of respect for nurturant and authoritative figures, a heightened awareness of fairness and conscience (superego) and a stronger gender identification with the same-sex parent.

In this dynamic, interactional struggle, the child seems to seek both actual and symbolic definitions of familial roles and their fullest meaning. Like the preceding quest for individuation or identity, the triadic oedipal struggle is by definition also laden with great tension for the child and parent; for there may be much uncertainty as to its actual outcome. This lack of certainty produces anxiety for the child, who will necessarily test circumstances and familial situations in order to provoke and thus to clarify response patterns and to understand relationship symbols.

The greatest negative risk of this phase occurs if the parents are quite divided and are not fulfilling each other's basic needs for comfort and intimacy. There is then a stronger likelihood that the child may be triangulated by the unstable spousal dyad, e.g., to enter into an alliance with one parent against the other. In such an instance the generational boundary is not appropriately maintained by the spousal dyad. The child believes that he/she has indeed mastered the family by displacing one of the parents. Such inappropriate realignment may thus imprint a skewed structural template or early introject of fundamental familial and human relationships. The child does not know his appropriate place in the scheme of things. He/she cannot belong fully to the peer subsystem while also being supported by at least one parent in a presumption of equality. If the emotional needs of parents are thus imposed too strongly upon the child, he/she will develop symptomatic behaviors which reunite the parents as caretakers of their new "problematic child."

While such a skewed alliance could occur with either parent, the displacement of the same-sex parent is particularly damaging, as it seems to engender for some children a confusion in sexual identification. For instance, the child cannot deeply respect and model from a parent over whom he/she feels innately more powerful or influential. Identification on a deep level with that parent would feel demeaning to the child.

Similarly, where triangulation of the child is permitted at this stage, the child does not establish a healthy sense of justice, fairness, and conscience. Instead, he/she learns, no doubt with a good deal of underlying guilt, that intrafamilial or political alliances are stronger measures for determining relationships than the natural bonds of affection, commitment, and appropriate intimacies. Whether the family resolves its developmental struggle at this phase in the direction of positive triadic relationships (where the child has both an authoritative and nurturant parent), or in the negatively triangulated form, the child's propensity to generalize family relationships to the environment helps to form its early worldview. The child may develop a sense of appropriateness and fairness, or may be lacking in these essential human values.

DEFENSE TRANSACTIONS

With the natural tension and anxiety of these early developmental phases and with the painful distortions, guilt, or even loss of primary relationships through poorly resolved affectional struggles or skewed alliances, defensive ego mechanisms will develop to protect the child from emotional pain. These dynamics, serving as a buffer or shield, also arise out of the interactional and relational context of the family, usually contributing to family homeostasis.

The child or other family members, who are unable to distinguish or to accept their own individual feelings and thoughts from those of others, may *project* or attribute these thoughts and feelings to others. This projective expression becomes a style of communication in the very enmeshed family structure, as family members presume to think, feel, speak, and act for others in the family. Differentiation or individuation is poorly developed.

Displacement occurs when a family member transfers the thoughts and feelings of one person to another, e.g., a child's presumption that one parent feels and thinks exactly like the other, or a mother's displacement of one child's emotions and ideas upon another child. Again, individuation and personal differentiation are underdeveloped in the family.

In the developmental struggles of the family there may be open *denial* of processes and feelings which are occurring. The unconscious processes of familial alliance formation, with its anger or guilt, cannot be openly acknowledged without threatening the structural balance of the family. Denial serves in the interest of maintaining the status quo, as does *reaction formation*, the substitution of one emotion, attitude, or action for the one actually in operation. Within the family context, *repression*, the pushing of anxious thoughts, feelings, memories, or behaviors into the unconscious, along with *avoidance* of situations which promote the memory of or the reexperiencing of the anxiety, protect the family from the great stress of change itself, e.g., the threat of realigning relationships, changing behaviors, and the ongoing developmental exploration of the unknown. Thus the classic defense mechanisms serve interactionally in the interest of the family system to ward off anxiety and prospective change.

Part II: Clinical and Service Implications for Syntonic Teams

As discussed, personality and intrapsychic process seem to develop largely from the interpersonal relationships that unfold within the family. The earliest dyadic bond between infant and mother promotes the psychological emergence of the individual and shapes the child's attitudes of trust and self-esteem. The young child's psyche, conscience, earliest projections of a worldview, and her/his understanding of powerful and nurturant relations are then further imprinted in the resolution of the triadic oedipal struggle with mother and father. Thus for the clinician to significantly enter into the interactional life of the family is also to become a part of the joint and individual psyche of its members.

An appreciation of the core concepts, especially the systemic dimension of the intrapsychic phenomena, will widen the clinician's scope of assessment, regardless of training and background, enabling strategic clinical planning for the family. The following areas become more available to the clinician in assessing the family:

1. Structural strengths or deficits; how appropriately are the subsystems formed and aligned?
2. Levels of individuation, self-esteem, and trust of the family members; does the family operate out of shame and fear or is there validation and free exploration?
3. Levels of nurturant and disciplinary behaviors; who provides these functions in the family and to what extent?
4. Gender identification; are sons identified with father and daughters with mother, or have their identifications been skewed?
5. Ethical views of the family; does the family operate out of a sense of fairness and honesty or in what ways do intrafamilial political alliances supercede natural affectional bonds?
6. Defense transactions; how does the family maintain its homeostasis; are denial, displacement, reaction formation behaviors operative within a triangulated system?
7. Pain or anxiety threshold of the family as a whole; what old hurts and guilts fester from interpersonal deficits?

For the traditional clinician whose primary aim is to enable the individual client to raise repressed material to consciousness, the broader systemic/intrapsychic assessment may seem minimally useful. The current interactional dance based upon the formative imprints will seem irrelevant. Likewise, the orthodox systems clinician, who focuses narrowly upon the current transactions of the family and sets no higher goal than the resolution of immediate symptomatic behavior, will find the deeper knowledge of the individual and family to be cumbersome and of minimal relevance.

On the other hand, intrapsychic/systems assessment is most applicable for the clinician who chooses high goals of personal growth for the client family, e.g., seeks optimal development of all members of the family. This clinician understands that movement beyond immediate symptom relief requires a resolution of some of the key issues arising out of personality formation. The client cannot move to higher levels of personal development and goal attainment if the painfully imprinted distortion continues to shape current familial and social transactions. Secondly, a working understanding of the core concepts will make it easier for the clinician over time to touch those early pains of the client, and, through deeper communication and positive transference, to provide a lasting corrective experience. The deficits incurred from skewed or inappropriate parenting, e.g., inadequate nurturance, discipline, or direction will need to be addressed and experienced in positive forms. The client will need to be able to discharge some of the early pain and to experience a powerful new relational context, which then enables current and future development.

In summary, the clinical framework described here is a *developmental*, or *formative* one. Treatment intervenes in the current transactional framework, with an appreciation of how the present system has been influenced by the spouses' families of origins and early transactional phases of personality formation. Systemic assessment and intervention foster realignments within the current context, relieving the immediate need for symptomatic behavior. On deeper levels the treatment offers a transferential or surrogate parental relationship over a period of time, resolving dynamic distortions and feelings and relational and affective deficits, through corrective experiences with selected persons.

While the private or facility-based clinician will usually engage in the therapeutic experience with the motivated, i.e., paying (usually middle- and upper-class) client family, the social worker and public agency professional more typically will work with nonpaying clients whose acting-out behaviors, e.g., child abuse and neglect, educational, delinquent, or criminal problems, require societal initiative and continuing responsiveness. For the latter clientele, special forms of outreach are required in order for enabling treatment experiences to be able to occur.

The vignettes in the alternate chapters of the book highlight families largely in the child protective and educational settings, requiring assertive intervention. In the child protective context, involuntary, societal interventions will provide essentially three options for the family: (1) to refuse service (sometimes necessitating child placement); (2) to comply superficially to the extent necessary to assure the child's safety and thus the eventual withdrawal of the service; or (3) to enter voluntarily a therapeutic relationship with the clinical social worker and team, after the compliance stage.

The key, then, to successful treatment and teamwork lies in the careful selection of team members who can provide those emotional and practical elements needed by the family system. The family must be able to sense that the selected team members are in close communication with each other and that they are addressing perceived emotional and concrete needs of the client family. When the configuration of the team, its makeup and what it has to offer, matches specific emotional and service needs of the family, and where possible, its cultural and ethnic background as well, it is truly *syntonic*.

Treatment, therefore, in a traditional facility-based clinical setting with a single therapist will not be acceptable for the vast majority of cases where initial involuntary outreach is necessary. In short, such cases require a higher level of voluntary participation and accommodation by the client than is possible. By contrast, the syntonic team accommodates to the family system, reaching out in the setting of the home and community in official, authoritative and nurturant ways.

While several types of teams will be described in Chapter

14 from a strictly programmatic or structural point of view, the therapeutic dynamics expressed by the social worker and syntonic team require further illustration at this point. For example, in "A Different Place" (Chapter 3), a vignette about a mother and family who change locations in both a physical and an emotional sense, the protective services social worker provides the initial service and therapeutic contact. Through investigative visits the service requires accountability of the family, sets limits around the abusive behavior, and introduces positive goals and possibilities for the mother and children. Within the transference the client reacts initially with avoidance and denial, but then agrees to cooperate with the service if the intrusive monitoring will withdraw later. The social worker's posture of firm support and positive expectation is in stark contrast to the client's childhood introject of a derisive father and absent mother and arouses the interest and later the emotional commitment of the client. From a practical stance the client considers not only what is expected of her but also the resources, both concrete and intangible, which are available to her in the service.

Addressing school problems provides relief of some of the extrafamilial or societal stress. The client now has someone powerful, who will also take her side at school. This benevolent parental-like person will hear her distress over her son but also will not tolerate her abuse of him. Indeed, the worker teaches her new and effective ways to listen to, to program, and to direct the child. The social worker over time becomes the idealized parent, who fills acknowledged personal and familial needs on both the intrapsychic and social, interactional levels.

The introduction of the family to well-selected educational and therapeutic services in the neighborhood begins the expansion of the service from a single worker model to the syntonic team approach. The new clinician, a black female like the client, will foster a nurturant and sustaining relationship in which the client will address her rape incident as well as early painful feelings and distortions arising from her childhood. The clinical social worker and neighborhood-based therapist become the nucleus of a cooperative, mutually supportive team. Modeling an effective, interracial relationship, they also become for the client in time the new structural and emotional introject which will profoundly influence the client in all of her developmental spheres—individual, parental, and spousal. Gaining strength and self-awareness, the client will, within the next few months, leave her own abusing paramour, until she is able later to enforce new standards in this relationship.

While the clinical social worker and therapist provide the deepest levels of therapeutic influence, interactionally and psychodynamically, the adjunctive members of the interagency service team, e.g., staff at the family shelter and the school, provide an emerging network of community support. This quite isolated client, who had seen her environment as essentially hostile and exploitative, is now able to discover a sense of community. With a family and community systems orientation, the team his resonated in response to primary social and emotional needs of the family. It is therapeutically, culturally, and concretely syntonic with the family system.

Finally, in "Getting the Drift," described in the vignette which follows this chapter, the clinical social worker initiates the syntonic team approach by reaching out to address concrete needs of the youth and his mother, specifically, helping the boy to earn money and assisting the mother to deal with her son on school-related issues. The deeper clinical relationship occurred with the boy, as his mother, who had not raised him and was not prepared ultimately to make more than a superficial commitment to him, was not available to the team.

In the transference the social worker touched the pain inherent in the boy's relationship to both of his parents. His depression was addressed by enabling him to acknowledge and to discharge some of his resentment and anger toward his father who had physically assaulted him, and to clarify specific distortion, e.g., that his father did not injure him because he, the boy, was "bad," but because the father was actually very angry on that day with his girlfriend. Later, after the mother made herself unavailable to the youth, the clinical social worker would enable him to express some of his grief concerning this relationship as well.

Through active outreach efforts, a working relationship

was cultivated with the boy's uncle, a competent individual, who was given direct and official support in assuming a surrogate parental role. This uncle, who had once been a probation officer, consulted freely and often in the initial months of service with the clinical social worker. Over time, this relationship demonstrated to the boy in a dynamic way how adults can work together in his behalf. Within this new triadic relationship, he seemed to experience a profound contrast to the parental models of his childhood. The boy resettled comfortably in the uncle's home, became an achieving student and found after-school and weekend .work in the community. Indeed, within this example, significant natural healing elements were cultivated within the child's own environment. The clinical counseling was brought into concert with indigenous resources (in this instance a stable, gifted member of the extended family), forming a team relationship with powerful impact upon the client.

In summary, the syntonic team approach described in these and a number of other cases referred to in this book has several distinctive features. Firstly, the team, composed of key professionals and, at times, mature adults indigenous to the child's extended family or community, will develop significant relationships with the child and family, *and with each other*, which provide corrective interactional and affective experiences for the client.

Over a period of at least several months, as trust develops, the new relationships create a structural template that challenges the faulty, inadequate introjects of early childhood. Through active counseling the child and parents begin to recognize distortions in their perceptions and communication skewed by early experiences in life. On affective levels the family experiences a greater sense of self-worth, independence, and personal achievement. A deeply nurturant figure is present on the team as well as another who may more often model structure and accountability, the two serving in the transference as optimal or "idealized" parents.

Within the behavioral dimension, symptomatic dysfunction is reduced or eliminated and new adaptive behaviors are taught, especially effective parental communication and discipline. Willing and appropriately chosen extended family members or family friends are engaged whenever possible to enable the service to be fully rendered, particularly where cross-cultural values are different.

In addition to the family systems and psychodynamic work, the syntonic team interacts directly with and on behalf of the client to relieve the stress of key dysfunctional service relationships in the community, e.g., with schools, welfare departments, legal or medical agencies. The systemic models of assessment and intervention are described more fully throughout the other theoretical chapters of the book, especially in the educational and social service contexts.

Lastly, whenever possible, the syntonic team will incorporate at least one key team member who is of the same racial/ethnic background as the client. The presence of this person, whether a professional or significant person indigenous to the client's social network, helps to assure that the service will be sensitive to the ethnic or cultural values and experiences of the client. This person will also provide the team greater access to the family and community network. Relating to such a team may also be the client's first experience of authentic cross-cultural relationships.

Chapter 11

GETTING THE DRIFT
A Vignette

Ms. Hirsh and her son, who are described in the following vignette, have built and maintained a secretive alliance in which they at first seek to protect each other from a hostile spouse/father and then from a presumably threatening social environment as well. By their flirtation with occasional responsible and competent behaviors and claims, mother and son hold the family service workers at bay for a number of months. Although it is not easy to "get the drift," pieces of the human puzzle begin with time to fit for the team. Some theoretical aspects of the transference phenomena and service delivery are discussed in the previous chapter. The child's uncle, a very capable man, works closely with the small professional team from the child protective agency and the school, ultimately becoming the child's surrogate father after the professional therapeutic services end. Through this important familial tie further placement is averted for the youth and his younger brother.

His head buried in his hands, Todd, a handsome 15-year-old black youth, sits on the steps of an alcove next to the courtroom where he will soon appear with his mother. He has heard his mother describe how he has failed nearly every subject in high school, largely because he so seldom attends. When he is at school, he often lingers in the cafeteria, cutting classes he does not like.

His mother, Ms. Hirsh, suppresses her anger as she speaks

about these things. Waiting to go before the judge for a routine review, she talks to me in the hollow hallways of the courthouse only about those things which she feels she must. It is information that could be easily corroborated anyway. Her life is full of secrets, and with this representative of the agency she does not know what parts of her past are known. Better to say as little as possible. Seldom belligerent at school, Todd simply refuses to go to many classes or to take most tests. Nor will he dissect animals in biology; he and his mother both feel squeamish, they say, about this matter. Once Todd wore a T-shirt to school given to him by his mother which shouted in silent print, "I don't give a shit." He was almost suspended on that occasion until he agreed to wear the shirt turned inside out.

Sometimes a teacher or counselor finds that Todd can be charming in his quiet, sheepish manner. But more often the school staff becomes quite frustrated with him and does not explore the reasons he is so depressed and withdrawn.

Probably Todd would not tell them even if they asked. What teenage boy wants to talk about the tragic personal assaults he has sustained on occasion from a drunken father whom he once hoped would care for him? Todd feels it is safer to speak in evasive parries now, if one must speak at all.

"Todd," I ask, "What kind of job do you want for the summer?"

"Dunno," he mumbles.

"What have you done before?"

"Cut grass in the neighborhood."

"Will you do this again this summer?"

"No. The lawnmower's broken."

"What would it take to fix it?"

"About forty dollars."

Todd feels he cannot ask his mother for money. Since she just left her second husband and has no source of income, and her welfare application has not yet been processed, she has enough daily burdens of her own. Ms. Hirsh has been with this man for seven years and has had two children by him. Todd lived with them for only a few months when this second parent breakup occurred. He feels some satisfaction, and yet somehow guilty. Perhaps the separation was his fault, he thinks, and now he has to be particularly loyal to his mother even though he has spent little time with her in his life. Hasn't she chosen him? Todd eyes his mother warily. He won't tell what he knows of her secrets if she will maintain the same favor for him.

"Todd, if you could get that lawnmower fixed, would you cut grass this summer?" I continue.

"Dunno. Other people have better lawnmowers—"

"What do you mean?"

"My neighbor said I couldn't cut his grass when I asked him. Then he let my friend with the new mower have the job."

"Your friend was a relative of the neighbor. You know that, Todd," his mother added, surprised at her own slip.

"What if you, your mom, or I could find some odd jobs for you to earn the forty dollars you need to get started?"

Todd's responses remain brief and noncommittal. His excuses, however, betray more self-doubt than hostility. He is not trying to get rid of me. If anything, he is baiting me a little. Who is this new person? How long will he be in the picture? Can he do anything for me, he wonders?

Todd is very interested in bikes. Soon after the court hearing I bring an old, rusty tandem bicycle to him for repair. His mother says she will help him keep a record of his hours worked and of the supplies he needs. Ms. Hirsh is not accustomed to someone reaching out in a tangible way, but she is visibly pleased this time. Todd also brightens up for a moment. He knows he can paint the bike and fix it up just right. Perhaps by this means his mother will allow me to get just one foot in the door, and I remind myself I should not expect more.

I leave the bike with Todd one Saturday morning and return two weeks later, after my vacation. Todd is eager to show me the transformation of the bicycle. His mother, however is not at home for this visit, although she knew I was coming.

During this first summer after her separation from Mr. Hirsh, she, Todd, and her two youngest children live together in a large boarding home. She has arranged with the proprietor that she cook for the residents in exchange for two rooms on the third floor and regular board for the family. I commend her for her resourcefulness, as there is almost no cash income nor public assistance grant for many weeks. Todd mops floors and runs errands for the proprietor. These tasks will become his summer job and help the family manage.

Increasingly, I note that Ms. Hirsh is not at home. A few days after such a failed visit, however, she calls the office excitedly. Panting for breath, she has run home from the park to her home. Todd was chased by two police officers, a male and a female. She happened to be crossing the park when Todd ran into her arms, ending the chase. The officers claim Todd has stolen a younger boy's bike; it is the same day she has refused to allow him to visit with his estranged father. The officers are pressing charges, and a policewoman says he has made obscene gestures at her during the chase. Todd adamantly denies all of these charges, but is hardly convincing to anyone, including his mother.

Clearly, Todd has pushed his mother into action, as she has finally become alarmed enough to respond to him in the community-based juvenile detention facility and asks for his return to her at court in a few weeks. He has engaged her. She is present for him at visits. Perhaps now she will make a commitment to him.

Awaiting his trial in the group detention home, Todd wins the approval of the director for outstanding and cooperative conduct. He makes friends with his peers, and his mother discovers a responsible paternal uncle who will also visit Todd and attend the trial.

It is not until many months later, however, that Todd acknowledges how he was trying hard to please his mother that summer while living at the boarding home. But he could not pull her out of her stupor—that distant world into which she drifted. He could not tell us then—nor would the proprietor break the secret—that she simply disappeared sometimes for several days at a time. They did not know where she was on those occasions—just drinking, they assumed. Todd was then left to supervise his eight-year-old sister and six-year-old brother, with a little help from the proprietor. Todd was very loyal in protecting the mother's secret as long as possible.

As the aging proprietor, however, tired of the children, Todd moved with them to a neighbor's home. Returning from one of her absences, his mother picked up the two younger children, later leaving the brother with a benign elderly couple who three days later turned him in to the police as abandoned. The child welfare agency would place this boy briefly. As the disclosure of events affecting Todd becomes somewhat more complete, mother and daughter cannot be found, although a friend of the mother's indicates that they are living together.

After this abandonment, Todd talks more freely about some of the crucial missing pieces. Over a year ago, his father, drunk and enraged, and claiming to have seen Todd walking earlier in the day along the boulevard during school hours, took a long, heavy board, hit Todd on one side and then the other until Todd's right arm was broken. When he was on the floor, his father kicked and stomped his chest until blood came from his mouth. For a long time it was too hard for Todd to talk about this shame—his broken arm and broken spirit.

He remembers being awakened a few hours after the assault by his 17-year-old brother who was living with his father also and who found him in his room. His brother took him to his mother's house where he stayed for several months before going back to his father. Later the brother came back to the father's house and beat up the father for this vicious attack against Todd.

Todd's mother carried him to the hospital on this occasion. Although he knew she had abandoned two of his younger siblings to an adoption agency years ago, Todd hoped against all odds that she would feel something for him now. Perhaps it would be different, since she understood his father's violence, having herself been its victim. She was glad to protect Todd for a while, but could offer little more, it seemed, than a roof and a bed.

Having shared his story for the first time, Todd shows me where his arm was broken by his father. I place my hand gently on the spot.

"Yes, it was wrong what he did to me," Todd reflects.

"And, how do you feel about it?" I ask persistently.

"Dunno," he replies. "I'd rather just go home and go to bed."

"Todd, you'll not go out of this room," I challenge, "until you first tell me how you feel."

"Yes, I am angry," Todd finally replies. "I had done nothing wrong. He was probably just angry at his girlfriend that day and took it out on me—yes, I am very angry about it!"

Staying informed about Todd's situation, his uncle, a stable, sincere man in his early fifties, invites Todd and his younger brother to live in his home with him. He has already taken in two other nephews, cousins of Todd, and established a full household. He reassures Todd and the agency that he has room enough, and that Todd has a family after all.

Through the six months of treatment, especially the gradual telling and retelling of his story, Todd has answered several basic questions for himself. He knows his father will destroy him (or anyone) who lives around his violent, alcoholic pattern. This fact does not mean that he cannot visit his father and even enjoy him on occasions. He expresses grief over his mother's abandonment, but is relieved that he no longer has the impossible task of taking care of her and his siblings. He learns to trust that his uncle will stand by him just as his social worker has. He realizes that he is not at fault for the pain he has suffered. Living with his uncle, Todd enrolls in a new school, attends regularly, makes new friends, and finds his summer and after-school jobs on his own now.

Chapter 12

CASE MANAGEMENT AND THE CASE CONFERENCE REVISITED
A Systems Perspective

Previous chapters have described specific interactional dances of the professionals and client family, as well as the clinical underpinnings of the syntonic and interagency team approaches. The purpose of this chapter is to review in greater detail the merits of effective case management from a systems or wholistic perspective.

Practitioners and researchers alike are focusing increasingly on the significance of the interactional behaviors of the professionals who themselves make up the service network and the ways in which their collaboration—or lack of it—affect the client and the client's family. W. Schwartz clearly delineates the social worker's role as not only to assist the client in his or her various personal and social relationships but also to enable the service system itself to carry out its appropriate functions:

> The social workers' skills are fashioned by two interrelated responsibilities: he must help each individual client negotiate the systems immediately crucial to his problems and he must help the system reach out to incorporate the client, deliver its services, and thus carry out its function in the community.[1]

Similarly, the specific interdisciplinary relationships that exist among the social worker and the other helping practitioners (including foster parents) are a matter of considerable interest in the literature. Both the inherent values and difficulties of these relationships are evident in such discussions, for example, those of the social worker and the lawyer,[2] the social worker and the police,[3] the social worker and the school personnel,[4-6] and the social worker and foster and biological parents.[7,8]

Especially in the field of child welfare, cases typically demonstrate a combination of several significant resource deficiencies, necessitating interventions by a number of social agents in such areas as employment, education, legal services, health care, housing, and counseling, among others. The client or family who seeks assistance with problems often finds it necessary to establish a number of different agency relationships over a period of time. This complex of services is the client's immediate social service network and the manner in which it is organized (or remains disorganized) appears to have a powerful effect upon the client's overall progress.

SERVICE NETWORK DYSFUNCTION

Although an effectively coordinated service network can ideally provide a rich range of resources, problems typically exist when there is an absence of effective coordination and collaboration. Types of problems include conflicting directives, values, and ideologies presented to the client from different social agents, including both overt and subtle miscommunications. Misunderstandings are unwittingly invited, it would seem, when a client who is already under stress is also forced to serve as the central switchboard for the various helping agencies, as in: "He said—She said—They wanted—" At times there may be direct competition among the services for clients' loyalty and involvement. In addition, the network's dysfunction often lies in the various providers' refusal to be aware of or to recognize each other's inputs and to avoid direct and ongoing communication. As Lee and Swenson[9] state:

"Social networks" refers to the field of significant interaction that a person (client) has—whether this be with primary group members, within voluntary associations, or with organizations or their representatives. The significant issue is that the parts of the ecological field are not necessarily in contact with each other.

If there is no coordinating social worker or case manager to assess the total operation of the client's service network, each service will have its own fragmented involvement with the client, who may well experience a continuing distress that maintains or exacerbates the presenting problem. In this sense the immediate social service network may resemble the disorganized family system, thereby operating as a damaging metasystem that impinges upon the family and individual. It is not uncommon to work with clients who feel (often correctly!) that they are the object of interagency scapegoating or power plays, that certain providers are uninvolved or uncaring, or that others are pulling them in conflicting directions, often with considrable pressure (as in some family court cases).

Covert and overt behaviors among professionals or helping agents denote such network dysfunction. For example, in abuse and neglect cases, a community agency or school, through bias or ignorance concerning child protective services, may seek to "protect" a child from the child welfare agency and a presumed risk of immediate placement by not reporting possible abuse in a prompt and legal manner. Necessary interventions and supportive in-home services may therefore not reach the family. In school cases, a variety of school and court personnel and parents are frequently engaged in conflict with each other, thus overlooking the concerns, needs, and capacities of the child. In other instances, well-meaning and progressive advocacy agencies may ally with distressed runaway youths or pregnant teens in ways that exclude the equally troubled parents and family from the process of joint resolutions and services. Such types of network dysfunction can at times promote even greater havoc for already distressed families.

Interagency service conflicts may also be quite subtle, for example, an agency's refusal to respond to correspondence or phone calls in a timely manner, or rigid insistence upon confidentiality procedures that exceed basic and appropriate legal requirements. Likewise, the presence of deep-seated cultural and professional biases among the professionals themselves may directly and negatively affect the collaborative process.[10]

CASE EXAMPLE: PROBLEM AND RESOLUTION

The following example illustrates how a client's aggressive ensnarement in a seemingly resistant service network can prolong a family crisis. The systems-oriented social worker, however, assesses the service network and intervenes in such a way as to promote the family's needs.

A single parent on AFDC, Ms. S. had been trying for 3 weeks before her initial visit to the community-based agency to retrieve her rebelling 13-year-old daughter, who had run away to the house of an adult boyfriend. Upon asking Ms. S. what other people or agencies were already immediately involved, the social worker learned of a court-related referral agency, two neighborhood police precincts, and the district attorney's office, among other agencies. Although the local police knew of this mother and daughter, they would not intervene on the mother's behalf without a written documentation of custody. The two precincts disagreed as to which was responsible. Ms. S. could not obtain the cooperation of the referring agency in acquiring the document. She had been to other agencies and no one was willing to help her. Apparently, as her desperation had grown, she became increasingly irate and accusatory, thus provoking reactions that she experienced as "getting the runaround."

Focusing upon the presenting crisis within the context of the dysfunctional service network, the social worker first called the court-related referral agency, which clearly had set up a double bind for the client; that is, they would help her to file the legal papers on behalf of her estranged daughter, but only if she could bring the daughter into their office for a joint interview—an impossible expectation under the circumstances! The new worker protested this contradictory requirement, and the agency acknowledged that in their frustration with the client they had assumed that the daughter was probably better off with anyone other than the explosive mother. The agency was relieved to learn that Ms. S. was interested in ongoing casework regarding her relationship with her daughter and that an agency was willing to accept responsibility for working with her. They then moved out of their obstructionist position, offering a simplified procedure for Ms. S.

When the worker wrote out the specific steps for the client, Ms. S. was visibly relieved that the system had reorganized itself in a reasonable way that she could understand. She experienced the successes of regaining her daughter within 24 hours and beginning a new relationship with the service system that could serve as a foundation for continuing help.

THE CASE MANAGER AS SYSTEM ORGANIZER

As this illustration demonstrates, a key to overcoming damaging and inherent network dysfunction lies in the worker's authoritative role within the network. This role is most meaningful when it can be conferred by the client as he or she develops trust in the social worker. The coordinating position may also be presented as a necessary requisite of the service and is demonstrated and explained to the client in the initial visits. In child protection cases, the role may be officially assigned by the family court, since the case manager is required to bring forward a service activity plan agreed upon by all parties. Thus, whether the central leadership role of the case manager is clearly voluntary or officially designated, the social worker ultimately seeks the client's cooperative involvement in order to reach the service goals acknowledged by the client.

The status of the case manager within a system of competing social work and/or non-social work agents depends upon several factors: (1) the will of the client (who either wants or does not want a coordinating social worker); (2) the conditions set forth by the agency (i.e., the agency may choose not to work with clients who do not want or support such a role); (3) or the sociolegal expectations placed upon the social worker (e.g., the public child welfare social worker who is either recognized or mandated by the family court to carry out the function).

The important issue is that a single social worker should be designated and given responsibility for the case manager role. If there is any dispute over this matter, the issue should be discussed in a case conference, particularly in light of the above three considerations. Generally, consensus can be reached as the specific roles of the participants are reviewed by all. If the misunderstanding is not resolved in this professional context, the client, in a voluntary arrangement, may have to make a choice, or in child protective or criminal justice cases, the court can be explicit about the role.

The coordinating case manager will focus upon the client's presenting issues and the client's social service context. First, he or she will determine all of the significant social agents currently or recently involved, the degree of their involvement, their behaviors/attitudes, and their particular goals for the client. Has the client been acquiring (or sending) conflicting messages among the providers? To what extent can the client be encouraged to resolve these issues on his or her own, and to what extent would the case manager's interventions be useful on behalf of the client?

After the service system's composition is carefully analyzed, a plan for intervention should be discussed and agreed upon with the client. The social worker sends out signed release-of-information forms and indicates in the cover letter the nature of his or her coordinating role. The social worker requests the cooperation of all relevant providers, their suggestions, recommendations, and case summaries, and also mentions the prospects of a case conference if necessary. In this manner the coordinating social worker further establishes his or her central position for the client in the service network.

As information arrives and contacts are established, the social worker assists the client in reassessing which service providers are currently essential and which are no longer significant. The particularly useful ones will be invited to the case conference attended by the client for the purpose of writing a coordinated service plan. The case manager will also discuss with the client before the meeting any additional services that may need to be included. This process serves to limit or expand the field of the system as needed and to establish boundaries. The randomization of service inputs can thereby be reduced and more coherence established in the transactions among the participants. This restructuring of the service system itself encourages all important parties to communicate openly and clearly with each other within an organized setting and with the knowledge of the client.

Where there may have been network conflict (overt or covert), the social worker takes on a mediating posture, promoting clarification of the various responsibilities of the social agents, encouraging questions and discussion, and focusing upon current goals and solutions. The social worker will discourage and interrupt blaming attitudes and behaviors.

By promoting direct transactions and organizing the communication flow of the various parties, the social worker relieves the client of the awkward switchboard function, which may formerly have screened and distorted information and relationships. As systems manager, the social worker monitors the overall delivery of services and, through necessary coordination, enables the client or family to work toward mutual goals.

CASE EXAMPLE: FOLLOW-UP

For the S. family, whose history continues below, a close-knit collaborative team of three essential helping professionals was developed out of the formerly chaotic client service network.

After regaining custody of her daughter, Ms. S. demonstrated trust in the original case manager and brought her daughter to the community-based agency for family services. Mother and daughter agreed that family therapy was a necessary additional service. A continuing exploration in this interview of the broader service system revealed that Ms. S. had been assisted in the past by a "family aide," a paraprofessional from a private child protective services agency from whom Ms. S. was now estranged because of an earlier explosive outburst. The social worker acknowledged the significance of this relationship and facilitated a reconciliation and resumption of this practical household service. Thus, the social worker, the family aide, and the new family therapist formed a successful, ongoing interagency team. In case conferences, the interagency team clarified their respective roles with the family, modeling for the family how a small system of adults can work together in a trusting manner toward mutual goals.

A fourth team member, a student lawyer, also joined the team briefly at a later point to help deal with a custody battle provoked by a paramour. The team continued for about a year until the family's system had stabilized.

Along with identifying and appropriately organizing the client family's immediate formal service network, the case manager should be alert also to the appropriate involvement of the informal network, that is, for example, relatives, friends, neighbors, and church. As the family introduces these persons, they too will be invited into collaborative efforts.

CONCLUSION

The significance of the service agents' relationships to each other and to the client—that is, the service network itself—cannot be underestimated and requires continual vigilance if meaningful service entanglements are to be avoided. As the client's immediate service network is organized effectively, the client's energies are freed up to focus upon resolution of problems. If further clinical work at the level of the client's personality and family structure is indicated, it too can proceed at this point with greater clarity and effectiveness.

Chapter 13

"ALL REASONABLE EFFORTS"
A Vignette

The family described in the following vignette demonstrates an uncon-
scious and sharp split between notions of "good" and "evil." The bridge
to respectability is elderly Aunt Jane, both for the religious and irrelig-
ious members of the family. However, the excitement, enticement, and
financial incentive of the parents' underground world of drugs and
prostitution, the very fast-track life of the urban ghetto, overshadow
Aunt Jane's religious influence and, to be sure, the family service pro-
gram, as well. Without criminal justice intervention, it is not possible to
develop ongoing relationships with the parents. Nevertheless, the inten-
sive in-home service illustrates a number of very positive attributes.
Genuine and well-coordinated outreach efforts are made to the family,
ultimately providing a critical safety net for the children. The three boys
will not be allowed to eat from garbage cans, to remain unsupervised,
to be battered periodically by mother or father, to play truant, or to en-
gage in bike thefts. Although in the background of the vignette, the in-
teragency team does in fact demonstrate a very high level of cooperation
among several social workers, child advocates, and the mother's attor-
ney, and provides very close monitoring of the children. Educational,
legal, housing, and other social resources are provided to the family.
And intensive therapeutic services, though rejected, are offered. Two of
the four children will be successfully cared for by Aunt Jane in her
home, and two of the older boys enter residential placement.

"Praise the Lord," the elderly woman greeted her caller as always, as she picked up the phone. Aunt Jane was a righteous, matronly individual with a mission to free her family, and the world, if possible, from the clutches of evil. If there was any escape from crime for the "unsaved members of her family," as she referred to them, Aunt Jane would point the way. She owned three small apartment houses and was well regarded by most people in the community. Her large extended family needed her resources and her respectability.

Tisha, her five-year-old grandniece, had been with her for several months now. Prior to arriving, Tisha had been with another aunt who could no longer care for her. This child had been away from her parents for three years. At the tender age of two, Tisha, a charming, healthy child, had been found severely beaten by her drug-addicted father, Joe. Tisha's mother, Evelyn, a prostitute, knew she could not nurture or protect Tisha and had agreed, though reluctantly, to the child's placement with the aunt.

Prior to my visit, Aunt Jane called on the phone to remind me, "Joe has served his time—three years for assault and armed robbery. He's different now. He goes to church. He sings in the choir. I want you to meet him."

At this our first meeting Aunt Jane's dashing young nephew was dressed in new, casual clothes; he was friendly, persuasive, and socially confident.

"In spite of what you've heard from others, I've changed," he said to me. "I'm working now as a delivery man with a firm. All I want is to make things right with Tisha and my boys." He would not request overnight or weekend visits with Tisha; he said he knew the system too well to even ask. But he would like to be able to visit Tisha at Aunt Jane's house.

Tisha sat close to her father on the sofa in Aunt Jane's old-fashioned parlor and then climbed up on his lap as he spoke of her. Aunt Jane had said Tisha would be all over him, "She likes her daddy and has forgotten about the past. She's a sweet child," Aunt Jane kept saying. "And she goes to church with me every Sunday."

Realizing that Tisha was still under protective court supervision and also feeling guilty about all those visits in her home she had already allowed on the sly between Joe and Tisha, Aunt Jane now hoped for agency approval. "Would it be okay if Joe visits her here?"

There was no reason to alienate Joe, and one could only hope that some of the aunt's good intentions had indeed rubbed off on him in the form of some positive behavioral changes. He was certainly entitled to supervised visits with Tisha. I responded very cautiously, however, for Tisha's sake:

"She does seem to enjoy being with her dad in Aunt Jane's home. Joe, I'd certainly like to believe in these positive changes. We're just meeting though. I'd like to get to know you—let's set up some appointments for that purpose."

Joe wholeheartedly agreed. He and Aunt Jane had carried off a wonderful meeting—a new beginning. Joe would be able to visit Tisha in this great-aunt's home on a trial basis with her direct supervision and with agency sanction.

Sadly, however, Joe did not keep further appointments and, before too many weeks, Aunt Jane began to reveal that he was "backsliding." She allowed him to visit Tisha until she realized that she was missing some valuable rings, and later a radio. He also stopped coming to church, she said. "Some people just can't stay converted," she lamented finally. "I think he's back with those bad people on the streets again."

In the meantime, I visited Evelyn and the three boys, Roy (eleven), Tom (ten), and Shareef (seven). At the initial afternoon meeting, Evelyn wore her evening best, a rose-colored chiffon dress with sculpted hemline and a deep-cut bodice. She welcomed me into her modest apartment with seductive courtesy. I was one of many social workers whom she had escorted through these dimly lit corridors, up the stairs, and past the living room, with its soft sofas and vases of arching fronds. A tattered window shade flapped over a broked pane of glass in the corner of her room.

We walked a little further and sat down at the kitchen table. Evelyn knew the arts of pleasing people and affirmed smoothly whatever might be expected of a "good client." She said she was attending an adult education class, and that it is never too late to educate oneself and to find a good job. The conversation focused, of course, on the boys. She couldn't understand why they weren't attending school. She knew they hustled money in the parking lot of the supermarket, carrying groceries for customers. They are not bad kids, she insisted, except perhaps for Tom, who stole a bike recently. She had him take it back right away and asserted that she had made sure to talk to the other child's mother.

I asked her if she knew about cord marks and scratches on Tom's shoulder which the school nurse had reported yesterday. Yes, she had seen some marks. She knew another child protective report had been made. Tom had shown the marks to her and had told her that he had been in a fight at school. "They certainly aren't cord marks," she replied calmly. "I would never hurt one of my children and I don't leave them alone like people have said before. They also don't pick through the trash. I always feed them." Evelyn acknowledged that she did worry sometimes when they were out of the classroom. She never saw Joe, she said. But probably the boys did meet him sometimes in the neighborhood during the school day—there was nothing she could do about this.

Together we discussed the purpose of the contracted in-home service which tried to provide two visits to Evelyn each week for a number of months. One visit was always announced, the other usually unannounced. She liked both women on the team who visited, she said, especially Mary Rose who had helped her learn a lot about taking better care of her money. She also had developed a good relationship with her neighbor, she said, who would watch her children if she had to go out for a little while.

I had met the in-home social workers briefly. Although they believed she was not leaving the children unattended, they felt there was little progress in other areas. The two older boys' behavior and school attendance were declining. Evelyn was months in arrears on her rent with the public housing authority and her time was running out before an imminent eviction would occur. She had also refused therapeutic treatment services which had been offered, and the workers knew she was not attending educational or vocational programs.

Arriving home from the grocery store one chilly fall afternoon, Evelyn found her apartment completely locked and boarded up. She had been evicted after violating a number of negotiated court agreements to pay her rent.

In a neighbor's kitchen at a quickly gathered emergency meeting of the team and relatives, including Joe, who reappeared after evading the professionals for some months, Evelyn pleaded, along with Joe, for a solution other than placement of the children.

After much discussion around the kitchen table with the mother's attorney, agency social worker, a child advocate, and the family, interim plans were made for the three boys to stay for a few days with another elderly relative. Various members of the team would visit on a daily basis while more stable plans were being developed. Aunt Jane then appeared, again coming to the rescue, offering her home and good intentions to keep the boys. She believed she could somehow manage to take charge of them. However, after two months of intensive effort and with considerable service support, she threw up her hands. Roy and Tom, the two older boys, were clearly beyond her control, engaging in bike thefts and life-threatening fights with other youths in the community. She and the team realized she could not succeed with them as long as their father Joe was seeing them on the streets and actively undermining her influence.

Roy and Tom entered a highly skilled residential child placement facility. Their mother Evelyn was picked up in the neighborhood for forging federal checks and was committed to a federal penitentiary. Tisha and Shareef adjusted successfully with Aunt Jane. Joe would be sought by authorities on new charges of burglary and selling of drugs, but remained indefinitely at large in the community.

Chapter 14

AN OPTIMAL FAMILY-BASED CONTINUUM OF SERVICES

Many dysfunctional interactional patterns of a systemic nature have been described in the context of services to families throughout this book, along with corrective treatment and case management measures. The present chapter outlines an optimal program continuum of family-oriented services including various forms of collaborative or team efforts. The service modalities vary according to the intensity of the client families' specific needs. Utilized thus far primarily in child welfare settings, the continuum could also be adapted to other family service settings, including community mental health agencies, youth probation services, or progressive school systems. The modalities may also be applied readily in either small or larger agencies, as the expertise and creativity of the professionals allow.

The emergence of services in many forms to children and families in their own homes in child welfare and family service agencies attests that this service can be highly successful in strengthening families who are experiencing severe emotional stress and a deficiency of essential resources and community services.[1-9] Although the intensive family-centered services are frequently home-based, aspects of the services occur in some instances within an agency's office.[10] As an alternative to institutionalization or substitute care, such services have also become an important cost-effective means for maintaining or

115

reuniting families.[1,5,11] Likewise, the 1980s reductions in social service funding—coupled with increasing demands for services to clients—have challenged public and private agencies alike to reconsider those indigenous strengths and resources that will promote children's permanency in their own families and communities, whenever possible.

In concept, family-based services offer casework and referral to those families who become known to the agency because they are experiencing a social crisis or serious family dysfunction. The services are intended to stabilize the family unit, alleviate conditions that present risk to the safety or well-being of the children, prevent placement, strengthen the family's capacity to function independently in the community, and improve the family's problem-solving and coping skills.

To conceptualize a working model of these services in a public welfare organization more clearly, a continuum of services—including carefully defined roles and requisite professional skills—was developed to correspond to a general range of clients' and families' needs, both with regard to the clients' psychological functioning and use of resources. The four primary categories of the family-based service include general case management, the comprehensive social worker, the in-house or *intra*-agency team, and the interagency team. These varieties of service focus with a greater or lesser emphasis on both therapeutic and social service needs of the family. Under each category, it is possible to define the primary roles of the social worker, the worker's basic activities with the client and the service network, and the skills needed by the worker for these functions.

Although specific cases are used to illustrate these general categories of service, it is important to emphasize that all cases simply approximate points on the continuum. That is, cases tend toward certain categories or directions based on the current configuration of families' psychological and resource needs as perceived by the social worker and supervisor. It is therefore the task of the worker and supervisor to reassess regularly the family's changing needs at both levels. Flexible service plans stating the mutual goals of the client and agency and the service components that are necessary are then developed with each family.

In those cases in which the family progresses successfully, it will move on the service continuum in the direction of more optimal functioning, including more independent, self-selected resources. Changes in assessment by the social worker, accompanying actual changes in the family's use of or access to resources (for example, gaining or losing a job), may significantly shift the position of the family on the scale of needs and requisite services. The practical value of the continuum is, therefore, to help the social worker and supervisor clarify the nature of the overall problem and the specific type of modality needed at the inception of service and at later stages.

GENERAL CASE MANAGEMENT

General case management focuses on helping to alleviate resource and social service deficiencies of the client by focusing on the client's contextual needs, for example, health, employment, or education. By relieving serious resource deprivations that are harmful to the children and family, that is, by fostering the basic social supports of living, the social worker seeks to strengthen the family in its own home and to avoid placement of the child. When the immediate caretaker of the child is assessed to be capable of carrying out the essential parental functions of psychological nurturance and discipline, the determination is made that the family does not require intensive counseling. The case of the Reid family, a protective services referral, illustrates how general case management was able to reverse a request for long-term placement.

Wynne, a deaf five-year-old boy, suffered severe neglect by his mother, who was a single parent. Neighbors had more than once seen Wynne wandering in the streets at 2 AM. After he had ingested Clorox on one occasion, medical personnel contacted protective services. A family-based social worker who was experienced at working with deaf children was assigned to provide the direct service.

Because the child's mother was unwilling to agree to counseling and to intensive services in the home, it was necessary to place Wynne in emergency foster care while a permanent plan was being developed. On investigating the situation further, the social worker discovered a grandmother who had originally indicated to protective services at the time of placement that she could not assume responsibility for this child because of his "difference": the child could not communicate, was unruly, and she believed him to be unmanageable. In talking further with the grandmother, the social worker found that there was less of an absence of concern than know-how on the grandmother's part. Therefore, the worker began to educate her about the special needs of deaf children. He also promised to make available to her the particular skills and resources she would need (for example, signing skills and admission for Wynne to a school for deaf children), if she would agree to provide a home for Wynne. In view of these new resources, the grandmother agreed to accept Wynne. He made a positive adjustment in her home and in the school, and he was spared the additional trauma of long-term placement.

The emphasis of general case management is on helping the client overcome severe deficits in resources through the coordination or provision of those social supports necessary for the child's growth and development. This social worker's skills, in addition to signing included the ability to listen well, to clarify and assess complex problems, to support and encourage the family's strengths, and to develop a feasible permanent service plan. His role was also to monitor the case for the court and to present regular reviews to the court for about a year. During this time, the social worker stood ready to reassess the case if the family's needs should change. If, for example, the natural mother were to seek meaningful reinvolvement with the child, services that included intensive psychological treatment might be indicated.

THE COMPREHENSIVE SOCIAL WORKER

For use of this service category, family behavioral problems must be particularly manifest; there may be one or more children who are acting out or symptomatic parents with alcohol problems or marital discord. Although serious deficiencies in family resources may exist, there are often sufficient organizing strengths or skills in the family that can be rather quickly marshaled to handle these needs with only a minimum of direct involvement by the social worker. The emphasis of this service category is therefore on activating more positive family functioning through family counseling. The social worker operates with the family primarily as a therapeutic agent and only secondarily as a facilitator of other resources.

The Smith's family's case illustrates how the SCOH social worker correctly assessed and treated an explosive family problem and thereby enhanced the family's capacity for enriching and utilizing other necessary resources as well. The Smiths were a multiproblem family who were referred by child protective services for voluntary assistance because of the family's inadequate housing and general disorganization. The social worker found at the first home visit a deplorable living situation for this family of a mother, father, and six children. There was, for example, no heat and no water in the house. Furthermore, because of the explosive nature of their relationship, the mother and father were unable to sit down in the same room together to discuss problems. The mother was embittered, yet passive, toward her all-controlling husband, and indeed much of their severe marital conflict had been triangulated to their 15-year-old daughter, who was acting out at school in noisy and, at times, hostile ways. Also in the family was a handicapped child and other children with health and school problems. The goals of the family-based service, as agreed on with the family, were to help make the house livable, to enable the parents to communicate better, and to assist the daughter in resolving her school problems.

To begin communication with the warring parents, the social worker felt that it was necessary for them to meet with her separately in the agency, which was conveniently located near their home. Over a period of some weeks, the husband began to exhibit a gradual trust in his wife's true capability, and the wife learned through therapeutic guidance from the social worker to approach her husband in more affirming and constructive ways.

As the marital and parenting relationship became more functional, the situation for the children, especially the 15-year-old, also improved. A crucial parent–child–school conference revealed that the child was quite angry in school because of peer pressure and her feeling that she was disliked because of how she dressed—an issue to which the parents were able to respond appropriately with the encouragement of the social worker. The worker also involved the girl in a modeling program at the neighborhood recreation center.

At the same time, Mrs. Smith began to demonstrate new resourcefulness in her relationships with the children's schools and other community and medical agencies. Mr. Smith actively improved the physical environment of the home, assuring also that the utilities would not be shut off again. In short, the resolution of the problems in the familial relationships enabled the family to apply its own resourcefulness and skills to solving a number of practical and more mundane issues.

A distinctive aspect, then, of the use of the comprehensive social worker mode is that the social worker is sufficiently skillful in family counseling and casework to focus on and to help change behavioral interactions within the family. The social worker generates effective interactional tasks or activities that activate more productive family dynamics. As an influential therapeutic agent, he or she seeks to nurture, to program, and to challenge the family to succeed in achieving specific goals. In general, improvement in the psychological functioning of the family enhances other latent strengths so that the social worker can often simply point the way for the family to any additional necessary community services that may be needed. Significant management of the service community is usually not required in such cases.

In-House Team

In deciding whether to use the general case management or the comprehensive social worker modalities, a conscious choice of focus is made during the assessment phase between coordination of social service resources or therapy; however, the in-house or intra-agency team concentrates intentionally and rather evenly on both areas of need. As experienced child welfare workers know, many cases exhibit powerful psychological distress *and* acute resource deficits simultaneously. Such cases contain considerable risk for children on both levels and will usually necessitate long-term placement unless intensive counseling and in-home services can be brought to bear in a timely and effective manner.

To address the full range of the children's and family's needs, it can be helpful to develop a two- or three-member intra-agency team with carefully defined roles. The team leader is generally the primary therapeutic agent who maintains general oversight and responsibility for the case. A second social worker concentrates more particularly on the important task of resource development and coordination with the family. This professional may also oversee the time-consuming court review process, if relevant.

A particularly poignant case in which such a team was effective is that of the Sterling family. After the death by cancer of their mother, who was a single parent, five teenagers aged 13 to 19 (two females and three males) were faced with the extraordinary challenge of maintaining themselves as a family or seeing the three younger siblings placed. At the request of an aunt and the oldest child Susan, who was 19, family-centered services were provided in an intensive manner to determine the degree of self-sufficiency of this young family. Unfortunately, the aunt's attitude toward the family was highly ambivalent and frequently negative, her own grief and long-standing hostility toward the deceased mother of the children impeding her effective involvement at this stage.

Family counseling and an array of adjunctive services were therefore provided by a two-member intra-agency team. The additional service activities included interventions at school, mediation with wary and sometimes hostile neighbors, advocacy with the public assistance office, a search for summer jobs and camp experiences, and the development of employment skills and referrals for Susan. For the first six months after the mother's death, the two social workers provided the intensive therapeutic and social service required for maintaining this unique family in its own home.

To promote Susan's personal maturity and also to relieve her of some of the weight of adult responsibilities she had taken on herself as "head of the household," in the seventh month of service this team also hired a paraprofessional family aide through an adjunctive service provider. The aide visited the home a number of times each week and served to reinforce the direction of counseling and other service tasks, for example, by encouraging Susan in negotiating reasonable standards, rules, and expectations with her siblings and in budgeting the use of the family's public assistance check. The presence of the aide also provided Susan with the freedom to focus on her own social life and personal needs more appropriately.

Through the intensive efforts of the intra-agency team and the later addition of a family aide, a number of crises within the family, school, and immediate neighborhood were resolved. The youthful family received the support and guidance they needed to begin coping with their mother's untimely death, and the threat of family disruption through traditional placement was successfully avoided.

There are several practical values to such an intra-agency team approach. First, each social worker has a clear and sufficient level of responsibility and need not become overwhelmed by the unrealistic expectations of providing all services to such cases. When deprivation and risk are considerable for the family, the team not only provides additional reserves for the family, but also provides support and encouragement to each other, exhibiting to the family how responsibility may be shared among several people. In this regard, the team also provides to each other additional perspectives on the nature of the problems and recommendations about what may be needed. Also, if one member of the team experiences difficulty in working with a family or family member, the second social worker may provide effective mediation. Needless to say, the success of such joint interventions will also lie, to a great extent, in the quality of the team members' relationships with each other and in the supports the team receives from their own agency, for example, ongoing training and effective supervision.

INTERAGENCY TEAM

The interagency team is clearly an important emerging modality for severely dysfunctional and socially and economically impoverished families. In addition to having serious deficits in resources, such families may exhibit extreme behavioral disorders, such as suicidal and homicidal tendencies, incestuous relations, or psychotic manifestations. The specialized therapeutic requirements of such cases suggest that it is often wise for the child welfare agency to engage appropriate family mental health providers directly. It is the family-based worker's role, then, to organize and facilitate the formation of a small, well-defined team of professionals and paraprofessionals (as needed) to develop a service plan. The three essential roles in this mode of service delivery are that of the case manager, the clinical family therapist, and the family aide. The emphasis of this category of service is on ongoing interagency collaboration with an intent to avoid long-term placement, if at all possible.

This approach carefully differentiates the leadership roles of the case manager and the family therapist for several reasons. First, the level of competence and amount of time required in the areas of therapy and social service development and coordination suggest the usefulness of specialization. For example, the singular task of developing and carrying out thoughtful and effective therapeutic interventions is usually considered to be a sufficient responsibility for therapists who are seeing a number of families. It is often not feasible, nor does the therapist generally see it within his or her role definition, to provide the full array of adjunctive services. Likewise, it is a skilled task and a time-consuming responsibility for the case manager to organize with the family an effective formal and informal network and usually a sufficient challenge as well, in view of the sometimes extensive caseloads of the case manager.

Second, if the case is under court supervision, it is often helpful for the case manager to distinguish, for the family's sake, his or her role as resource coordinator and court representative from that of being the therapist as well. At times it is indeed possible for the highly skillful social worker (the comprehensive social worker) to be both a significant therapeutic agent and a court monitor. However, when deep levels of trust and confidence are required, the more nurturant therapeutic relationship may be more easily fostered when the roles of therapist and court monitor are filled by different people. Thus, the likelihood of negative transferences from one role to the other can be somewhat diminished.

Although it is not uncommon for a case manager in many traditional settings to refer a family to therapy, it is important to emphasize that the work of the interagency team goes considerably further. The work of the interagency team is characterized by a continuing or ongoing relationship between the family-based worker and the clinical therapist over a period of some months in their common commitment to strengthening the family unit. Thus, the case manager and family therapist develop mutual service goals with the family and other relevant parties. The team discusses in a consistent manner—usually in the form of regular case conferences—operating procedures, values, service activities, and significant therapeutic changes in clients.

The third important team role is that of the family worker or family aide, usually a paraprofessional from another agency who provides practical day-to-day support to the family for a critical period of time. The aide may, for example, go shopping with the mother, accompany her on school visits, instruct her on infant care, or help her to establish a household budget. If the family is initially anxious or resistant to family therapy, the aide may transport or accompany the family to sessions and serve as a trusted and influential surrogate family member for a limited period of time. Thus, the aide is a significant contributor to the team and, through inclusion in the case conferences, receives encouragement and direction as well. In this manner, the aide's differentiation from the family is protected, thereby enabling eventual separation, when this aspect of the service may no longer be needed.

With a former history of brother—sister incest and more current symptoms of alcoholism and family violence, the Evans's case required careful monitoring and specialized interagency team intervention. The team consisted of the case manager, the clinical family therapist, and the family worker or aide.

Ms. Evans was a single parent with an alleged history of criminality and child abuse. She had three children living at home, two in placement, and adult children living away from home. Ms. Evans had had innumerable contacts and relationships with social agencies over many years. But because her style was at times abrasive or explosive, as after drinking bouts, many service providers had stopped trying to assist her.

When she presented herself to the community-based agency with a request for help in retrieving her runaway daughter, Ms. Evans' parental rights and responsibilities were affirmed, in spite of her history, and a trusting relationship was developed. Service interventions were able to help her regain her teenage daughter, and a service plan was developed that included family therapy and other adjunctive services. During this initial phase, the case manager organized an interagency team consisting of a clinical therapist, a family aide, and himself. The aide had had previous contact with the family through a service that had been interrupted. The case manager provided a central coordinating role for the next 12 months. This role included meeting with Ms. Evans on the average of twice a month, accompanying the family to court and presenting the court with a service plan, facilitating a number of case conferences with the entire team, and assisting as needed. Other services included intervening with the public assistance office and with schools as well as arranging for legal services.

The family was seen by the family therapist on a weekly basis. As progress was made in issues of setting boundaries and establishing more appropriate roles, the teenage daughter stopped running away and became somewhat less "parentified" (being treated as a parent rather than a child) by her mother.

In turn, the family aide provided many practical supports to the family in visits, which occurred once and sometimes twice a week. She also accompanied the family to appointments for treatment and reinforced therapeutic goals.

Progress was made in helping Ms. Evans to experience

somewhat higher levels of parental and personal functioning and to use community resources more effectively. The safety of her own children and of an infant born to the adolescent, conceived by the teen during the original runaway episode, was carefully monitored.

Despite a stressful three-month period involving the family's poor adjustment to the newborn that did, in fact, necessitate a brief emergency mother–infant placement, long-term placement was avoided, and the family was reunified. Despite the family's highly complex problems, there was consensus that progress was made and that a baseline of self-sufficiency was reached.

In sum, the team's activity involved a number of case conferences and direct discussions concerning members of the team's roles and expectations for each other. Each team member handled at least one emergency with the family on behalf of the team. There were, of course, numerous telephone calls during crisis periods, and all three team members were present for several crucial family sessions. When the original family therapist moved out of town in about the eighth month of service, the case manager and family worker provided continuity for the service team until a new clinical therapist was assigned.

Without this intensive intervention by the interagency team, it is unlikely that the children would have been able to remain in their home in the long term. Nor would ongoing personal growth have been likely within the family if the more radical action of immediate placement had occurred. It is more probable that if this traditional route of placement had been used at the beginning, considerable alienation between Ms. Evans and the child welfare service would have resulted and that the client would more likely have used every means to sabotage the placement. In view of her history with agencies, she may well have succeeded in frustrating placement or any other goals and in reaction may well have placed herself and the children well beyond the reach of effective and necessary services. Instead, the family experienced considerable support and significant influence from the interagency team.

Conclusion

According to the working model presented here, family-based services can be a viable and comprehensive program for maintaining and strengthening families which exhibit severe and multiple problems. Services may be rendered in several ways with greater or lesser emphasis on therapeutic intervention or social service coordination and court supervision, depending on the comprehensive needs of the family, the level of risk to the children, and the professional resources and skills available to the child welfare or family service agency. A full assessment of psychological and service resource needs of the family enables the family service social worker and supervisor to appreciate the scope of the problem and its threat to the children and thus to select the appropriate modality for each family. Well-defined modes of service delivery provide clarity to the family concerning the operation of the total service and promote breadth and efficiency.

Chapter 15

MADONNA OF THE PARK
A Vignette

*Having settled for several months in a nurturant foster family, the two
primary children in the following vignette, Richard and Ramika, are
visited by their young, attractive mother, who had previously abandoned them in a mother–infant shelter program. This mother exhibited
a serious alcohol problem, was mildly retarded, and largely controlled
by strong negative influences in her extended family. Family-based services were unable to penetrate the defensiveness, hostility, and alcoholic
patterns of the larger family, where exploration of the child's sexual
abuse in a high-rise housing project and subsequent life-threatening
trauma were not fully resolved.*

*The family service program is in the background of this vignette
which is told from the young surviving boy's perspective. Some elements
of the story are reasonably assumed from the child's treatment context
and from what was able to be documented in the original investigation.
Successful collaboration with the foster care agency led eventually to
these two children's adoption by the new foster family, after their mother
discontinued regular visitation. This vignette describes the poignant dilemma of a family where sensitive treatment and placement services
were essential for the children's safety and continued well-being.*

Behind the young family, Canadian geese swam unnoticed in
and out of the tall marsh grasses of a broad, quiet pond. The
green suburban park provided a grassy bank for the family's

visit, their first together outside of town since the children were abandoned by their mother and entered foster care.

On a blanket thrown on the park lawn, Alison, an attractive young mother, sat with her petite two-and-a-half-year-old daughter, Ramika. The child, like her mother, was silent and tentative. Not having seen this gentle woman for four months, Ramika was not entirely certain now who she was. She nevertheless felt strangely familiar to her, and she noticed how her older five-year-old brother, Richard, called her "Mommy." Ramika looked to Richard for further cues. He was obviously quite happy to see this "Mommy," as he romped around them both, as well as a boyfriend and a new baby. This kind woman seemed safe enough, and Ramika knew they belonged together somehow. The mommy's face was pleasant and her touch soft, though not entirely steady, as she cuddled Ramika in her arms.

After chasing his shadow for a long while, Richard finally tumbled down beside them, trying to catch his breath. His large, round, wide-set eyes looked intently at a new baby sister, to whom his mother's boyfriend had just introduced them. Perhaps the new baby is the reason his mother has been away for so long, he thought. Richard wondered if the baby would also come to live with Ramika and him. Would he need to protect her too? Or would the baby stay with his mother, keeping her away from Ramika and himself again for many months? Too many hard questions were now racing through his mind, and he began to feel more and more restless. He tried to forget them all; there would be time later perhaps to ask for the answers. Richard looked wistfully at the new baby's glistening black hair and minute fingers, and wondered if he himself was ever so tiny.

Richard wished the boyfriend were not there today. He remembered how the boyfriend lashed out at him on other occasions. He had also heard him shout at his mother about not putting up with those "stupid people" who kept bothering them from the "agency." Richard did not know what the word "agency" meant, but thought it must be related to the fact that he could not live with his mother. He wondered if this boyfriend also hit his mother like the last one had. She seemed afraid of him. As the questions piled up inside his mind, Richard jumped up suddenly and began running around again. He would not tumble until he exhausted himself.

In the past, Ramika and Richard had been brought into the city for visits. Today was unusual, though. They were surprised to see her out here in their own new neighborhood. Before, Richard had never been sure at the end of the long ride into town if his mother would even be there. Many times he had to wait for her to arrive in that room full of the amazing toys and little chairs. Several times she had not arrived at all. Then a fury like a sudden storm came on him and he would kick all the stupid people around him who were, he thought, keeping his mother away. Why shouldn't he break a few heads off dolls and throw crayons around the room? Why wasn't his mother there those times when he wanted her so much?

At those angry moments, the bad dream often jumped into his head again, very suddenly, although he knew he was not sleeping. He imagined Jim's angry hands picking him up by the shoulders, lifting him, then throwing him down—down —down. Why couldn't his mother at least *be* there, when people said she was coming? It had always been this way, since he could remember. Even before Jim got inside his head and into his sleep.

Today Richard told himself he would not be so angry. Could that be what was keeping her away? The park was a good place to be, and his mother was there, even if for a short time. He lay very still, pressed against her side, and thought about the long open-air hallways in the tall housing project where he had once lived with her. Often he had peered through the fencing along the sides of the hallway and had imagined himself to be a bird flying through the sky. He remembered how tiny the buildings seemed to be below him and how the people on the ground looked as small as the roaches that crawled on the walls of their apartment. Richard thought about the dark, smelly elevators that carried him up to these magical heights, and how his slightly older brother Tommy had told him not to be afraid and had helped him stretch up to push the number 13 button.

Richard admired Tommy very much and was sure Tommy knew everything there was to know in this world. Tommy had also taught him where to hide when the kids played hide-and-seek. He helped him not to be so frightened when smoke frequently billowed up from the trash chute into the hallways. He and Tommy had dropped old bottles and cans into the chute many times. He enjoyed waiting with Tommy, counting the seconds until their bottle landed with a crash into the incinerator below. Many times Richard and Tommy had seen the much bigger boys also drop matches into the trash chute. Soon smoke would come from the chute, filling the hallway and slipping under the door into the empty main room of their apartment.

At times Richard thought the pictures in his mind were like the thick smoke. They could become very blurry. As hard as he tried he could not remember exactly what had happened that last crazy night at home—that night when grandmom's strange boyfriend Jim was his baby-sitter. He knew it was very late and that his mother had gone out. She said she had to go to the store. She always "went to the store" when she was shaky. He knew if he were still awake when she returned there would be that smell on her breath.

Richard remembered how on this night he cried for her not to leave, although it would do no good. He cried because he knew grandmom's boyfriend was no real baby-sitter like the other baby-sitters he had had. Richard was very scared of Jim but still he couldn't let his mother know what Jim would do when she left. He had liked the candies and treats Jim had given him for a while, but he did not like falling asleep with his face in the old man's lap. Did Tommy know what Jim was doing to him? Tommy was supposed to know everything.

On this night something was different. Tommy had not gone to sleep when Jim came into the room. When he heard a noise a few minutes later, Tommy jumped up, turned on the light, and started screaming. Jim was caught off guard and was scared stiff. He just wanted the screaming to stop fast. Falling around and trying to pull up his pants, Jim turned the light out again and quickly locked the door. Jim was breathing very loud and making sounds. Richard could see his shadow over Tommy; he was hitting him and telling him to shut up, shut *up*, shut *up*!

Richard was not sure what happened next. He thought

Tommy was rolling around trying to get loose. Then just as suddenly his crying got soft and faded away. Then, it was quiet. Where was Tommy? "*Tommy!*" Richard wanted to scream. But he kept still as Jim grabbed his shoulders and lifted him up to the window. He didn't fight. The smoke billowed back into his mind. Richard fell asleep for a long, long time.

When he woke up finally in that strange pale blue room they called a hospital, people kept saying it was a miracle. Richard had never heard the word before. He looked for Tommy to tell him what they meant. But Tommy wasn't there. Richard wondered why everyone acted surprised that he was alive. Of course he was alive. But they said Tommy was with God now. Richard knew that that night Tommy had flown far away into the sky.

Now people kept asking him what had really happened. He could not say anything. Even the police came and asked him questions. Richard said he did not remember anything— not even the angry hands. Besides, he didn't know the words to say it even if all the smoke had blown away. Jim was at the police house. But Richard wondered what difference that would make.

Richard was glad his mother stayed with him in this hospital room after he woke up. But she looked very sad and had the smell on her breath. He thought she must have been to the store for a long time.

Even his baby sister, Ramika—he called her "Mika"— didn't make his mother happy now. They moved together with his mother to a house in the country, with other mothers and children. Although the people there were very kind to all of them, his mother kept leaving—just when he wanted her—just when his mind got a little less smoky. Why did she keep going away for such long times? He couldn't find out.

Maybe it was her way of giving Ramika and him a new mommy and daddy. Was that what was happening? His mother met the new mommy and daddy for the first time today, before they came over to the green park. Richard was very glad they had all finally met each other and were friendly. He didn't feel so bad for liking his new mom and dad now, since his old one seemed to like them too.

Richard lay very still in the dark grass of the park holding his mother's hand tightly. He wondered if his mother would be back again. But that was something not to ask. He watched the geese swim smoothly on the pond.

THE ORGANIZATION UNTO ITSELF

A Commentary on Organizational Dysfunctions, Complementarity of the Problematic Organization and Family Systems, and Strategies for Change

Having discussed a number of common interactive dances between the professional and client family at the casework level —both those patterns that are unhelpful as well as some that contribute to meaningful family-oriented services, it is important finally to examine more closely the large and very complex service organization itself. Clearly what the helping professional can accomplish with clients is to a very significant degree dependent upon the structure, functional dynamics, and overriding values of the service agency, i.e., the behavioral context of services to families.

Just as the client family operates according to its established systemic rules, attitudes, and roles, the human service agency is also governed by operational modes requiring adaptation and efforts toward change by the professionals operating within it. Not surprisingly, the hurdles and obstacles that impede change, effective programming, and client treatment are legion. Thus, committed human service personnel in conjunction with other progressive social forces have always necessarily sought ways in which to intervene in and to correct the most difficult systemic problems. Indeed, many of the conceptual and service modes described in this book have developed from such struggles within the service context to improve the quality of the organization and services to clients.

The purposes of this concluding chapter are then (1) to highlight some rather classic organizational characteristics or dynamics that impede successful service, (2) to examine the systemic behavioral and attitudinal complementarity of the problematic organization and the client family, and (3) to consider the broad outlines for promoting further positive change in the service organization.

Although many of the behaviors and traits are recognizable in various forms in small service agencies, this chapter is directed more particularly toward large bureaucratic social service institutions. And though they are of course serious matters, I have also lightly coined them the "dirty dozen" dysfunctional dynamics—acknowledging that change in any organization's way of functioning or providing services should begin with a sensitive, nonblameful recognition of problems in the agency's life sphere.

THE "DIRTY DOZEN" DYSFUNCTIONAL DYNAMICS

While the large human service organization espouses helping clients through various forms of assistance or direct services, its internal operations and interactive behaviors at times suggest more compelling priorities. An analysis of the bureaucratic system indeed indicates an array of characteristics and dynamics that may contribute to a general malaise in which stabilization or maintenance of the status quo becomes foremost. Twelve particular systemic traits—the "dirty dozen" dysfunctional dynamics—are briefly described; these include: exclusivity of function, the closed system syndrome, mutual client-staff collusion, homeostatic rigidity, turfism, triangulation, passivity, negative rewarding, minimization and denial, racism and sexism, narrow unionism, and pseudo-professionalism. Each of these behaviors or attributes contributes ultimately to the exacerbation of the client's presenting problems, thereby creating a poorly served client population that sometimes becomes dependent over several generations.

EXCLUSIVITY OF SERVICE FUNCTION

Exclusivity of service function is a status conferred by the public usually through government mandates to particular human service organizations. Entrusted neither to grass roots efforts nor to the private sector, certain key services are, for example, publicly institutionalized in order to address major needs of clients, including income compensations, housing, education, or direct personal services to children or families.

When the public sector agency is so designated, it offers to the citizenry at large a convenient mechanism to which it may summarily refer a host of social and human problems. The referring agent assumes then that he is being responsible in referring people to such resources. Unless, however, the referring source is also encouraged to actively enagage, when appropriate, in the service process, the ongoing helping responsibility and useful potential of the referring source may be overlooked or denied.

Wittingly or unwittingly this unfortunate situation displaces family and community involvement, particularly when the public agency is encouraged to assume full responsibility for very complex, multidimensional social or family problems, i.e., problems arising in a social or community context. The taking on of this exclusive function or role may obviate the potential input of willing helpers; or if they are, on the other hand, eager to be excluded, it exonerates them, especially when they may be a significant part of the presenting problem.

In the area of child protective services, referring sources from the community often choose, because of fear or lack of knowledge, to have little to do with the client family after the referral, even if there is a prior relationship, e.g., neighbor, teacher, pastor, friend. When the child protective agency likewise requests or expects nothing of a referring source, or even turns away offers by the source to help, it takes on a responsibility beyond its means and is from the outset often doomed to fail. The creation of this exclusivity may derive from society in general, from the agency's posture, or it may be considered to be the result of the collusion of the client or referring source with the service organization.

Further, this process of exclusivity is enhanced by misunderstanding or misapplication of confidentiality regulations. While the professional or *mandated* child protective reporter, for example, who is in an ongoing relationship with the client, may legally be informed of the outcome of an investigation and may be invited to assist in service planning and service implementation, the formation and utilization of a service team is frequently the exception rather than standard practice. Similarly, the nonprofessional reporter is often excluded from follow-up and engagement unless the social worker is well trained in systems or network interventions, knowing how to work through the client to involve other key parties.

The practices of exclusivity may maintain agencies which are by design severly overwhelmed. One needs to work in the areas of public services such as housing, public assistance, public education, family court, or family social services for only a brief time to begin to appreciate the necessity of appropriately engaging all capable and interested parties who have important relationships to the client toward the joint resolution of significant problems. Clients will, by and large, welcome such collaborative engagement when it is presented as a standard form of joint responsible services, and when they themselves help to identify their range of resources.

In sum, exclusivity is the presumption of the organization's total responsibility for the resolution of complex client problems. Such a position places the client and community in a diminutive posture, neglects to empower the client to assume major responsibility within the larger social system, e.g., learning how to get a job or to negotiate within social and educational settings. It clearly overlooks the utilization of the client's extended family and community network. Unfortunately, it is the modus operandi of many large public and private human service organizations, indeed, a major operational dilemma of increasing proportion in the modern welfare state.

CLOSED-SYSTEM SYNDROME

Placed in a defensive posture by unrealistic expectations of society, the organization may instinctively close itself off from the wider public. In this way, exclusivity of function often leads to tight organizational boundaries expressed in a general restrictiveness of communication between the organization and community. This closed system syndrome is characterized by a relative absence of creative, interactive communication between professionals inside the organizations and persons outside of the agency. There is little perceived need for interdependent work or relationship, and the notion of active interagency collaboration around cases or policy issues is essentially foreign. The utilization of outside trainers or consultants will be minimal; in the worst instances an administration will be threatened by such contacts, and their utilization by employees will arouse suspicions of disloyalty to the organization. Less controlling and more secure agencies will tolerate some interplay with professional counterparts from outside the organization, although considering such activity to be of little relevance. Participation in professional conferences, joint research, or other broad-based professional endeavors will be discouraged.

Thus the closed organizational system presumes an unrealistic omnipotence in a given service area, at times managing public or private funds and a monopoly of services with only routine accountability to other agencies. Exclusivity of function and the closed-system syndrome are therefore based upon an underlying defensiveness—sometimes a siege mentality where great expectations are placed by a public that also abdicates much of its responsibility.

Within such monolithic, closed organizations will often be found enormous pent-up frustration, an intolerance for the discovery of new ideas, and ultimately a climate of despair and hopelessness. Overwhelmed by the enormous and impossible task placed upon itself, such entropic systems at worst conclude that there are no solutions to the problems they are mandated to solve whether it be unemployment, homelessness, public education, care of elderly people, or the protection of abused or

neglected children. Hopelessness supported by rigid organizational maintenance of the status quo may breed a climate of
cynicism and depression within the organization.

MUTUAL COLLUSION

Mutual collusion is the agreement between the professional and client, usually tacitly, to ignore the underlying problem and to be satisfied at best with a very temporary "solution."
It is a short-range and shortsighted plan which will require the
reentry of services in the future as a matter of course, thereby
creating continuing client dependency. In its most extreme
form it is the client's and professional's agreement to avoid a
relationship and needed services altogether.

For example, a homeless dysfunctional client may have obtained, through the public agency, a few nights' stay in a boarding home of even a woefully inadequate apartment in a dangerous, poorly kept public high-rise building, only to return in
a few days or weeks with a similar need. Or an acting-out or
abused child may have been stabilized through removal of the
child to a placement setting, while leaving at home potentially
vulnerable siblings. If effort is not made to resolve the parent–child dysfunction, the same serious problems will again
erupt when the child returns home within a few months or
years, or another child will be scapegoated during the first
child's absence.

Also, in the area of individual or family treatment collusion may exist, once a presenting symptomatic behavior is
eliminated. A child's fighting behavior may abate at school as a
result of short-term treatment which enhances some family
communication and more effective parental behavior. If the
parents' unresolved marital issues or a substance abuse problem are a deeper basis for the child's acting out, the symptomatic behavior will generally return in a short time, assuming
these treatment issues are not also addressed.

Of course, such service or treatment agreements to "stop
while we're ahead" are not necessarily detrimental if there is
also a true commitment between the professional and client to

work further on any new problems in the future. However, too commonly these "gains" are questionable at best and the client revolves in and out of the service system, usually changing workers each time a new problem presents itself. Thereby the client family further establishes a career of dysfunctional behaviors and a multigenerational dysfunctional relationship with the agency.

HOMEOSTATIC RIGIDITY

Homeostatic rigidity is a characteristic of the closed system which maintains order and constancy at all costs. The organization does above all what is comfortable for itself and what seems to least "rock the boat." Where professional assignments are made at high levels, for instance, the appointed executive especially understands the cardinal rule of "making no waves." In its most extreme manifestations client services may appear to be incidental to the organization's perceived right to exist and to operate unto itself. In addition, the maintenance of conformity operates as a defense mechanism, protecting staff from a myriad of repressed emotions.*

Stabilization of staff problems, rather than resolution of them, contributes to rigid homeostasis of the organization. Creative change and policy development, which could arise out of problem recognition and resolution, is supplanted by other avoidance processes. If the professional in such a static system is, for instance, demonstrating a problem in a given location, the problem is seldom addressed. A problem-solving process which would allow for problem identification, the expression of feelings, concerns, and professional developmental needs, or the creation of new procedures, would be unbalancing to the system. It is therefore more comfortable to transfer the individual or the problem to another part of the large organization. This shift may occur repeatedly and serves the function of relieving tension (i.e., restabilization), albeit temporarily.

* While homeostatic process is a natural and at times positive phenomenon of human systems, the author is discussing here the extreme rigidity which retards or refuses to allow necessary developments and adjustments to occur.

Reorganizing large groups of staff sometimes appears to work in a similar manner. However, the reassignment of staff or administration without the change of leadership practices does not, by and large, affect the modus operandi of the organization. Therefore, these changes too often are external in nature and do not produce the intrinsic developmental growth which the organization needs.

TURFISM

From the higher-level alignments arise complex divisions of control within the larger service system. The span of control of the appointed administrator extends to the strict number of staff under this person. And the maintenance of these numbers requires a protection of turf, often with little relationship to actual service needs or client service demands.

Turfism usually does not allow a person to transfer across divisional lines unless there is a one-for-one exhange of positions. Since service demands are secondary to the maintenance of the "fiefdom," some assigned staff may at worst have little work to perform while other divisions, e.g., emergency intervention services, are overwhelmed with responsibility. When expectations are not equitable among staff, the overtaxed will become further disenchanted, and seek reassignment. Simultaneously, the underused portion may become demoralized.

TRIANGULATION

Along with turfism, mutual collusion, and the closed-system syndrome, organizational triangulation also serves in the interests of rigid homeostasis, undermining necessary change. It is a three-party dynamism in which two of the conflicted parties relieve the anxiety of their predicament, especially that which would be produced through open conflict, by labeling a third party as "the problem." This process may select completely innocent professional victims (or clients, as discussed in Chapter 2 and Chapter 4). It may create symptomatic scapegoats within the organization who perform according to the negative expectations of the two collusive parties; or it may overreact in very harsh ways toward a party, e.g., an underachieving staff person, who may merit only moderate reprimand or correction. The urgency of the unacknowledged conflict seems to determine the severity of the triangulated response within the service system.

The victim(s) within the organization may stand out because of his particular differences, whether strengths or weaknesses, in knowledge or functioning. Ironically, if the professional distinguishes himself as too highly capable with clients, if the individual's work standards and expectations exceed the norm, and if the high achiever promotes these standards among others, perhaps upon entering a new appointment, a collusion may well occur between staff and/or administration to seek to demote or sabotage the individual. Attempts may also be made to discredit good work as irrelevant or inappropriate or even to malign character. Without a sufficient political base, the achieving professional can be vehemently undermined.

Similarly, administrative triangulation blames supervisors or workers, individually or in groups, thereby refusing to address real issues and problems within an agency. In this way, an administrative level avoids confrontation, communication, and intrinsic change within its own ranks at all costs. In these common collective manifestations, the scapegoated party is accused of incompetence. And, indeed, these qualities may be simultaneously programmed into supervisors or workers who are not given proper assignments, effective supervision or training, or where low expectations are held from the beginning.

PASSIVITY AND CONFORMITY

While triangulation within the organizational setting is most visible in its aggressive forms, it is often accompanied by extreme passivity or conformity as well. In this context passivity is the disdain of responsible involvement, often based upon the professional's insecurity, lack of interventive knowledge, or conditioned fear of repercussion in the present or future. In its most insidious forms passivity gives permission to another's demise.

Commonly, passivity rests in depression. Individuals or groups may have long ago decided that they are powerless and therefore will not speak out jointly. They may be angry with the abuses they have experienced in the service organization, exasperated by its claims, and disillusioned by its failures. Extreme conformity to the climate or ethos of the organization creates, however, a repression of vital feelings, e.g., fear, affection, anger, gratification, resulting in future isolation and depression.

The aggressive leader is quite aware of the latitude afforded by organizational passivity. Indeed the most severe forms of triangulation occur when the peers or supervisors of the scapegoated party have resigned themselves, permitting organizational abuse of other colleagues or subordinate groups. If there have been other previous disputes between the triangulated individual(s) and those who could provide an alliance, passive aggressiveness can be particularly vindictive. Of course such processes can operate within and among any of the levels of the bureaucracy.

NEGATIVE REWARD

This dynamic overlooks recognition for accomplishments or may overtly negate achievement. It is essentially a controlling device which serves as an equalizing and homeostatic mechanism and is expressed in many subtle as well as more direct ways. Negative rewarding occurs in the public human service system when, for example, a professional who makes an outstanding intervention with a client, instead of being recognized by the supervisor is overwhelmed with another more difficult assignment. Indeed, the over-assignment of cases and the absence of either built-in rewards or external incentives, including appropriate salaries, is highly damaging and tends to negate professional self-esteem. If, for instance, the worker carries an excessive number of cases, there will be no incentive to complete and to close cases if the social worker is to be "rewarded" with an equal number of new and more difficult ones. From this vantage point, excessive caseloads build in the necessity for a certain percentage of "deadwood" or inactive cases, which the professional feels that, for his own protection, he dare not close. Therefore to urge the closing of cases without assurances of some total caseload reduction becomes a form of negative reward, promoting inactive service to large numbers of registered cases.

MINIMIZATION AND DENIAL

Minimization and denial are in a sense coping behaviors within the service organization and the larger society that overlook the scope or severity of very complex client problems. Problems are therefore conceptualized and addressed in narrow, fragmented ways, as various services, or service divisions, for example, compete separately for the client's time around interrelated issues, e.g., employment, education, housing, or psychological counseling. A wholistic assessment of the client's developmental phase and ability to utilize any of the services effectively may be needed, rather than the randomized approach.

Also, when public funds for service agencies are restricted by fluctuating state or national priorities, clients may suffer greatly. Staff shortages and the public organization's frequent inability to pay for the most highly trained professional personnel are accompanied at times by popularized opinion that suggest many clients are not truly deserving of services after all. Such forms of minimizing and denying at all levels of the service system and society at large provide a strong defense against meeting the seemingly overwhelming needs of clients and become a justification for other organizational or societal priorities.

Racism and Sexism

Within the human service organization, contemporary racism and sexism occur whenever unhealthy alliances of control are established along ethnic, racial, or sexual lines, whether black or white, Hispanic or Asian, male or female. Although alliances that are client-centered may be quite constructive, e.g., directed toward fair professional representation of a given client population, internal organizational alliances too commonly act as vehicles for advancing their own ethnic or same-sex professional members, regardless of talent, experience, or clients' requirements.

Client service is greatly affected by such biased internal divisions. The disservice is most evident in the transfer of cases from one worker to another or from one part of the organization into another section where racial dynamics are destructively at play. The client will be denied service continuity between the previous and former professionals who managed the case. At worst, a biased professional will discredit another professional in communication with the client, thereby promoting confusion or hostility for the client in his relationship either with the new or old worker.

Narrow Unionism

Unionism has become a mixed blessing for many human service professionals.

To the extent that demands from an administration are inappropriate, particularly with regard to working conditions, space, time, salary, and benefits, enlightened unionism has enhanced the professional status of public human service personnel. In urban settings, unionized public employees tend no longer to be so grossly underpaid as formerly and, as a result, more highly trained personnel will remain longer and provide more effective services.

However, by "narrow unionism" reference is made to the

organized effort on the part of workers in the service sector to perpetuate positions and benefits for their own sake and without regard for the service needs of clients. It can perhaps be one of the strongest of all the stabilizing or rigidifying dynamics, as, in its extreme forms, it may assert the professional's right to defy creative expectations of supervision or administration, regardless of their practice efficacy.

Unfortunately, narrow unionism will ardently oppose any shift of expectations, including service improvements, if these directions are not popularly supported. Such oppositions to progressive practice will be undermined, without strong and united counterbalances of supervisory and administrative levels or the backing of public policy. If, for instance, a supervisor or administrator proposes higher or more sophisticated levels of professional functioning, the individual(s) advising such changes will meet active opposition. Since narrow unionism is quite aware of the administration's need for orderly routine (a dynamic ripe for exploitation), it will find sufficient administrative support, usually covertly, to undermine change. At its worst, triangulation of progressive professionals, often at the supervisory level, will occur through such covert administrative-union alliances.

PSEUDO-PROFESSIONALISM

Lastly, pseudo-professionalism serves as a defensive barrier to genuine engagement with clients or other professionals in the service community. This phenomenon utilizes external status as a primary determinant of behavior and response and may become authoritarian or coercive. Prescribed, routinized, and rigid behaviors are substituted for appropriate, spontaneous, skillful, and compassionate interaction with clients.

A classic example is the emergency worker who, after seeing several hundred severe crises, has become seemingly callous to all. He will walk through the motions of service, such as collecting intake information, but miss the human element. Such distanced behavior understandably defends or insulates

the helping professional from constant exposure to human suffering that may be a regular part of the job.

If he has not felt gratified through previous experiences,
and if the organization itself provides a stressful, rather than
supportive environment for the professional, pseudo-professionalism or the rote operation of one's organizational function
will become a dominant, defensive means of "surviving" on the
job. Such behaviors are often endemic in some sections of the
service organization and are maintained through a number
of the various homeostatic functions which have been described.

In conclusion, the public human service organization, often overwhelmed by the enormous problems derived from the
inappropriate exclusivity of its function in society, may lack,
without significant external inputs, the orientation, commitment, or technical problem-solving expertise to address the
serious problems it is mandated to solve. Rather it may readily
institutionalize means and methods that maintain first and
foremost the status quo. Through these "dirty dozen" dysfunctional dynamics, which comprise by no means an exhaustive
list, the isolated, monolithic human service organization often
operates as a powerful entity unto itself.

THE FAMILY-AGENCY COMPLEMENTARY PARADIGM

As described in previous chapters, the human service organization interfaces with a network of related groups and individuals, forming around each client family a particular configuration and interplay of behaviors. Likewise, the sponsoring
human service organization itself and, for the purposes of this
discussion, the large bureaucratic human service agency, is engaged in a distinctive service dance with each of its client families. Where there is commonality of values and attitudes and a
complementarity of behaviors between the poorly functioning
organizational system and the family system, the outcome is
more likely at best to be short-term stabilization, followed by
continuing episodes of family malfunction and service contact.

As noted, a revolving door of services occurs and a pattern of service dependency may be carried on over many years and frequently from one generation to the next.

In contrast, effective treatment and resolution of problems occurs when the systems-oriented professional or syntonic team is able to engage in a significant therapeutic relationship with the family, while at the same time skillfully orchestrating the family's own personal, multifaceted service network.

Complementarity of the poorly functioning family system and an inadequate organizational system is reflected attitudinally and behaviorally. In this dysfunctional configuration— usually the most common—the underlying attitude on the part of the family *and* the human service professional is hopelessness and despair. The family feels that it has tried every means it knows to resolve the behavioral problem, usually described as a child's difficult conduct. The parents ultimately believe that there is no real answer to their dilemma, no actual means for relieving their anxiety and those behaviors that pervade and disturb the family's life.

The presenting family is typically very uncomfortable among themselves with constructive discussion, indeed does not begin to know how to disengage from the destructive behavioral patterns and to engage positively in problem solving. Its means of coping with stress therefore are usually to label the child as the problem, and to program the child to become behaviorally symptomatic.

In the dysfunctional family–agency complementary paradigm, the human service professional also has given up hope and has despaired. He has seen few, if any, examples of meaningful resolution to severe conflicts and may not be fully trained in problem-solving modalities, particularly in effective psychodynamic and family contextual models. And he is ultimately very uncomfortable with the notion of engaging the family in an intimate treatment relationship. With the avoidance of a uniquely corrective relationship the professional is quickly seduced by the family system, as he perceives the family's problems through eyes not dissimilar from the family's own. Underlying issues and conflicts therefore do not surface and are poorly defined, if raised at all. Communication and the relationship itself are generally superficial. Both parties have substantial feelings of doubt, and mutual distance is maintained.

Either of two negative behavioral outcomes generally results from this mirroring of common underlying attitudes, feelings, and behaviors. The first of these complementary patterns emerges from passive dynamics of the agency and reflects the family's own neglectful patterns. Overwhelmed by caseload demands and in a context of doubt, mistrust, and insecurity, the professional may simply neglect a case that does not loudly demand attention. If the child, for example, is not at imminent physical risk, and the family is quite resistant to services, as may often occur, the case will be overlooked.

In one case, that of the Almany family, the parents had separated a year before but continued to live in the same neighborhood while maintaining an active feud with each other —often through their fifteen-year-old daughter Carla. Carla's loyalty was thus torn between both parents as she moved back and forth, literally, from one parent's residence to the other. Neither parent provided nurturance; neither established parental control over Carla, and neither allowed the other to do so. Not surprisingly, Carla's acting-out behaviors escalated as she increasingly played truant from school, stayed out all night at unknown persons' homes, experimented with drugs, and, in a matter of a few months, became pregnant.

Because of the parents' history of neglect of Carla, a petition had been filed some months previously by the agency which allowed the social worker to monitor and to report to the court Carla's situation. The option of comprehensive family-oriented treatment had not, however, actually been offered to the family by the agency's human service worker.

Overwhelmed with his caseload demands, and lacking sufficient training, the human service worker did not wish to be reminded by his supervisor of the scope of Carla's problems nor that there were both legal and effective treatment options available for her and her family. The direct service professional chose rather to minimize and to rationalize by asserting that Carla was simply going through a rebellious teenage phase. Indeed, he cited that since her recent pregnancy she was showing somewhat more cooperation toward her mother.

Investing in a meaningful working relationship was an unsettling and frightening proposition for the professional and he became exceedingly resistant to the supervisor's recommendations and urgings.

Having had a previous working alliance with the supervisor's administrator, the direct service professional successfully sought his support in an effort to close the case. An inappropriately optimistic report was then made to the court by the worker based upon a few weeks of relative stabilization by Carla in her mother's home, and the case was summarily discharged from the court and closed by the agency. Pursuit of quality treatment by the supervisor had actually created for the worker a *destabilizing* dynamic, which was overruled by unsupportive administrative input. In this manner the family system and the service system became complementary—each contributing to the maintenance of the family's dilemma, to Carla's acting out, and to the rigid homeostasis of the organization itself.

The converse of neglectful service occurs when the professional is drawn too deeply into the family's aggressive or hostile rejecting patterns toward its own members. Here again both the family and the human service professional operate from the common belief that there *is* no viable solution to the dilemma.

In the Wallace case, eleven-year-old Jamie, an only child, had been subjected to very rigid and harsh discipline by his single-parent mother. When the mother's demands became too great, her manner too overbearing, or her threats of placing him too distressing, Jamie would run away, first to neighbors, and later to his maternal grandmother's home. Triangulation within the family occurred when the grandmother sided with Jamie, and thereby undermined the mother's role—e.g., she would comfort Jamie and not even tell his mother that he was at her house. In this context of unresolved hostility between the adults in his life, Jamie would also run from his grandmother's, and eventually was brought by the police to the agency for services.

Labeling his mother abusive, the assigned professional sided with Jamie and recommended immediate placement.

The worker presumed little hope for the possibility of the mother, grandmother, and Jamie resolving their conflict, nor was family treatment actually provided. With the family's consent, placement, on the other hand, allowed for stabilization to occur at least for brief periods. When Jamie inevitably returned home, however, conditions and behaviors remained the same and the disruptive cycle was repeated many times. The internal conflict of the family was maintained unwittingly in this way by the agency. A deviation by the social worker away from this cycle of intervention to genuine family-based problem solving would not have found agency support, and may have jeopardized the professional's status. Again the placement service was complementary to the family's dysfunctional system.

In summary, both the neglectful agency response and the more aggressive response demonstrate complementary behavioral patterns in which the service system interplays with the family's style in such a way as to preserve the status quo of both systems and to avoid resolution and real change. Both agency postures collude with, rather than challenge, the presenting hopelessness and despair of the family. There is a tacit agreement that the problem—often not fully assessed and identified—is nevertheless unsolvable. The neglectful response underutilizes the resources of the agency and community, e.g., the child and family may "fall between the cracks," not being heard from again, or reappear in a much more desperate condition in the future. In the other response mode, temporary stabilization is reached but expensive agency resources are grossly overused through the continued repetition of the placement cycle.

Toward Humanizing Services

The corrective treatment modality which enables the family to move from its destructive, patterned behavior is characterized by a strong sense of hope that conveys to the family that their presenting problem is indeed solvable, that meaningful familial and community relations can develop through their participation in a viable comprehensive service and particularly through their involvement in a therapeutic treatment relationship that offers new meaning and direction. Espousing such a view and training the human service professional to provide treatment interventions to the family in the context of a fragmented professional community would require, however, a period of intense destabilization within most large service organizations, if it were to be considered at all.

Although some critics would argue that significant change in the human service organization is impossible, it is this writer's belief that an effective change process, though fraught with struggle, could occur through several possible channels, including sophisticated citizen advocacy efforts, expert consultation and training initiatives, client group pressure and, above all, the joint working alliances of committed professionals inside and outside the monolithic structures, especially in client-centered work.

Citizen Advocacy Efforts

Genuine advocacy groups are needed to operate as vigilant monitors of specific human service areas, concentrating not only on fiscal and legislative policies affecting the human services, but also on the internal workings of the key organizations. Because the human service agencies are greatly influenced by higher-level board or political appointments as well as by a political tone that opts for stability at all costs, the effective adovcacy group will need to organize in a manner that states its position fairly and dramatically in the public arena.

Developing ties with progressive elements within the large service organizations, advocacy groups can gain legitimate access to both organizational plans and general service activity. Consider, for example, an organization's attempt to cut off funding to a highly successful experimental program because of shortsighted financial expediency. A well organized advocacy body that recognizes the political process of the organization, and is also knowledgeable of such special programs and the creative efforts of committed professionals from within the

service system, can indeed stand well poised to intervene supportively.

Such groups can also lobby forcefully for enlightened
high-level executive appointments, insisting on the assignment
of outstanding professionals who will implement major program reforms above narrow political gains. In such a case the
advocacy group should anticipate with the new organizational
leaders, a period of organizational transition and destabilization and be prepared to demonstrate ostensible support for
leaders who promote quality services for clients.

Moreover, an effective advocacy group, in order to maintain its own credibility, must scrupulously avoid any funding
source that would compromise its independence. Likewise,
through its bylaws, it must question and, at times, deny mem-
bership to present or past leaders of the organizations who
might infiltrate the advocacy system, regardless of how distin-
guished or influential such persons may be. If such leaders are
indeed on the side of progressive developments within the human service institutions, not simply defenders of the status
quo, their help can be most valuable through diplomatic efforts
from within the system at points of stress in the change process.

In summary, the effective advocacy group which would
hope to influence large human service organizations must be
willing to maintain high visibility, to lobby, and to pressure
publicly for needed reforms. It must be staunchly independent
in order to hold credibility and fair-minded rather than blaming in its approach. Also, it must maintain active communication with progressive, committed professionals within the service organization it is trying to assist, thereby rallying to their
assistance through either quiet diplomatic means or public outcry when necessary. Such an alliance is critical to counterweigh
the regressive trends discussed in this chapter which vigorously
oppose humanistic, client-centered change in the service organizations, and the concurrent and inevitable destabilizing transition period which accompanies positive changes.

Client Group Advocacy

Although clients serviced by large organizations are often relatively poor, disorganized, or fragmented, certainly there are precedents of successful client-organizing efforts, particularly in advancing certain housing, public assistance, and public educational reforms. In the area of personal services, e.g., mental health or child welfare, the client advocacy effort may develop direction, identity, and cohesiveness out of the context of group treatment programs.

As member constituency matures and becomes better informed, it will address issues of client rights and concerns. In addition, its own progressive momentum will, at times, provoke some adminstrative attempts to cut back or eliminate the group work program, as it becomes destabilizing in its clamour for change. At this point the client group may need to become politically connected outside of the organization and to lobby publicly in order to establish itself as an integral and ongoing client program. Support from citizen advocacy groups will also be critical at this phase.

Staff Training

Consultation and training has generally focused upon enhancing direct service modalities. It is usually in large service bureaucracies limited to rather random inputs by a gamut of unrelated training providers—a potpourri of theories and modes. Such training approaches, however, aside from the value of providing staff with a refreshing diversion from their daily routines, have little ongoing impact upon the ability of the staff to provide quality services to clients.

On the other hand, a commitment on the part of an agency to shift to a significant long-term family and community treatment mode would necessitate the identification of training providers who are appropriate and who are available for 2 to 3 years of systematic training and consultation for all levels of staff.

The starting point of such training would be the supervi-

sory level and would require supervisors to also carry a few direct service cases, in order to fully grasp and to internalize the
new treatment approaches. This step is critical if supervisors
are to be able to support and to reinforce their own professional staff. Indeed, their training must begin in earnest before
the training of direct service staff can commence.

The selection of training and consultation resources should
be based upon their proven and effective experience in other
settings. The training provider should be able to document
how services have promoted successful problem-solving modalities with clients and substantially reduced patterns of recidi-
vism. An active consultation component by the provider is also
important for special consideration of administrative issues and
concerns.

Clearly, the training approach as a vehicle of organizational change is the most straightforward and orderly means. It
can only occur, however, with enlightened, committed leadership and with the ongoing support of external citizenry or client advocacy efforts. It is thus a tertiary intervention.

In the final analysis, the change process within the large
human service organization will be slow, especially in the urban
context, and will be contingent upon carefully orchestrated
efforts of professionals and citizen advocates from outside
working with committed professionals from within the service
agency. This work together most often and most importantly
begins in the client-centered casework process itself. It may also
occur in the other organized advocacy and training efforts described.

Lastly, it is this author's hope that such a coming together
would eventually shift the predominant organizational forces
from the rigid maintenance of the status quo—the organization's apparent existence unto itself—to a new position dedi-
cated first and foremost to clients' needs and their successful
treatment through the collaboration of appropriate resources
from all sectors of society. Since many of these service organizations are owned and officially legislated by the citizenry itself,
it is all the more important to recognize the opportunity of a
creative working together of the key participants in a society
which historically espouses an enlightened democratic process.

REFERENCES

CHAPTER 2

1. Auerswald, E. H. Interdisciplinary versus ecological approach. *Family Process*, September 1968, 7, pp. 205–215.
2. Hoffman, L. & Long, L. A systems dilemma. *Family Process*, September 1969, *8*, pp. 211–234.
3. Bryce, M., & Maybanks, S. *Home-based services for children and families*. Springfield, Il: Charles C. Thomas, 1979.
4. Hartmann, A., & Laird, J. *Family centered social work practice*, New York: Free Press, 1983.
5. Compher, J. V. The case conference revisited: A systems view. *Child Welfare*, September–October 1984, *13*, pp. 411–418.
6. Jurkovic, G. J., & Carl, D. Agency triangles: Problems in agency-family relationships. *Family Process*, December 1983, *22*, pp. 441–451.
7. Emerson, R. *Judging delinquents: Context and process in juvenile court*. Chicago: Aldine, 1969.
8. Miller, W. B., Baum, R. C., & McNeil, R. Delinquency prevention and organizational relations. In *Controlling delinquents*. New York: Wiley & Sons, 1969.
9. Miller, W. B. Inter-institutional conflict as a major impediment to delinquency prevention. *Human Organization*, Fall 1958, *17*, pp. 20–23.
10. Aponte, H. J. The family-school interview: An ecostructural approach. *Family Process*, September 1976, *15*, pp. 303–311.
11. Compher, J. V. Parent, school, child systems: Triadic assessment and intervention. *Social Casework*, September 1982, *63*, pp. 415–423.
12. Tucker, B. Z., & Dyson, E. The family and the school: Utilizing human resources to promote learning. *Family Process*, March 1976, *15*, pp. 125–141.

157

CHAPTER 4

1. Schur, E. M. *Radical non-intervention: Rethinking the delinquency problem*, Englewood Cliffs, NJ: Prentice-Hall, 1973, p. 167.
2. Matza, D. *Delinquency and drift*. New York: Wiley & Sons, 1964.
3. Emerson, R. *Judging delinquents: Context and process in juvenile court*. Chicago: Aldine, 1969.
4. Platt, A. M. *The child savers: The intervention of delinquency*. Chicago: University of Chicago Press, 1969.
5. Wheeler, S., et al. Agents of delinquency control: A comparative analysis. In *Controlling Delinquents*, S. Wheeler, (Ed.). New York: Wiley & Sons, 1968, pp. 31–60.
6. Schur, ibid. pp. 164–165.
7. Aponte, H. J. The family-school interview: An eco-structural approach. *Family Process*, September 1976, *15*, pp. 301–311.
8. Tucker, B. Z. & Dyson, E. The family and the school: Utilizing human resources to promote learning. *Family Process*, March 1976, *15*, pp. 125–43.

CHAPTER 6

1. Aponte, H. J. The family-school interview: An eco-structural approach. *Family Process*, September 1976, *15*, pp. 301–311.

CHAPTER 8

1. Billingsley, A. Family Functioning in the low-income black family, *Social Casework*, December 1969, *50*, pp. 563–572.
2. Dodson, J. E. Black families, the clue to cultural appropriateness as an evaluative concept for health and human services. Paper presented at the Black Experience Conference of the School of Social Work, University of North Carolina, Chapel Hill, North Carolina, February 1981.
3. Gitterman, A., & Schaeffer, A. The white professional and the black client. *Social Casework*, May 1972, *53*, pp. 280–291.
4. Canino, I. A., & Canino, G. Impact of stress on the Puerto Rican family: Treatment considerations. *American Journal of Orthopsychiatry*, 1980, *50*, pp. 535–541.
5. Mizio, E. Impact of external systems on the Puerto Rican family. *Social Casework*, February 1974, *55*, pp. 76–83.
6. Vazquez-Nuttal, E., Avila-Vivas, Z., & Morales-Barreto, G. Working with Latin American families. In *Family Therapy with School Related Problems*. Rockville, Maryland: Aspen Systems Corporation, 1984, pp. 75–90.

7. Mostwin, D. In search of ethnic identity. *Social Casework*, May 1972, *53*, pp. 307–316.
8. Kim, B.-L. C. Casework with Japanese and Korean wives of Americans. *Social Casework*, May 1972, *53*, pp. 273–279.
9. Keller, G. N. Bicultural social work and anthropology. *Social Casework*, October 1972, *53*, pp. 455–465.
10. Green, J. W., & Leigh, J. W. The structure of the black community: The knowledge base for social services. In *Cultural awareness in the human services*. Englewood Cliffs, NJ: Prentice-Hall, 1982, pp. 95–121.
11. Montalvo, B. Home-school conflict and the Puerto Rican child. *Social Casework*, February 1974, *55*, pp. 76–83.
12. Devore, W., & Schlesinger, E. G. *Ethnic sensitive social work practice*. St. Louis: C. V. Mosby, 1981, pp. 133–158.
13. Jenkins, S. *The ethnic dilemma in social service*. New York: Free Press, 1981, pp. 3–40.
14. Schermerhorn, R. A. *Comparative ethnic relations—A framework for theory and research*. New York: Random House, 1970, pp. 20–35.
15. Norton, D. G., et al. *The dual perspective: Inclusion of ethnic minority content in the social work curriculum*. New York: Council on Social Work Education, 1978, pp. 3–10.

CHAPTER 10

1. Lifton, R. J. *The life of the self: Toward a new psychology*. New York: Basic Books, 1983 (see esp. p. 41 & pp. 29–81).
2. Breger, L. *From instinct to identity: The development of personality*. Englewood Cliffs, NJ: Prentice-Hall 1974.
3. Freud, S. *Standard edition of the complete psychological works of Sigmund Freud*. James Strachey (Ed.). London: Hogarth Press, 1953–1956.
4. Piaget, J., & Inholder, B. *The psychology of the child*. New York: Basic Books, 1969.
5. Erickson, E. *Childhood and society*, New York: Norton, 1950.
6. Bowlby, J. Separation Anxiety. *International Journal of Psychoanalysis*, 1960, Vol. 41, pp. 89–113.
7. Mahler, M. S., Pine, F., & Bergman, A. *The psychological birth of the human infant: Symbiosis and individuation*, Basic Books, 1975.
8. Bateson, G., et al. A note on the double bind—1962. *Family Process*, March 1963, *2*, 154–161.
9. Haley, J. *Problem-solving therapy*. San Francisco, CA: Jossey-Bass, 1976.
10. Hartmann, A., & Laird, J. *Family-centered social work practice*. New York: Free Press, 1983.
11. Hollis, F., & Woods, M. E. *Casework: A psychosocial therapy* (3rd ed.). New York: Random House, 1981.

12. Kirschner, D. A., & Kirschner, S. *Comprehensive family therapy. An integration of systemic and psychodynamic treatment models.* New York: Brunner/Mazel, 1986.

CHAPTER 12

1. Schwartz, W. Social group work: Interactionist approaches. In *Social work encyclopedia* (16th ed.), Vol. 2. New York: National Association of Social Workers, 1971, p. 1258.
2. Bernstein, B. E. Lawyer and social worker as an interdisciplinary team. *Social Casework*, September 1980, *61*, pp. 416–422.
3. Parkinson, G. C. Cooperation between police and social workers: Hidden Issues. *Social Work*, January 1980, *25*, pp. 12–18.
4. Aponte, H. J. The family-school interview: An ecostructural approach. *Family Process*, September 1976, *15*, pp. 303–311.
5. Compher, J. V. Parent, school, child systems: Triadic assessment and intervention. *Social Casework*, September, 1982 *63*, pp. 415–423.
6. Tucker, B. Z., & Dyson, E. The family and the school: Utilizing human resources to promote learning. *Family Process*, March 1976, *15*, pp. 125–141.
7. Pike, V. Permanent planning for foster children: The Oregon project." *Children Today*, November–December 1976, *5*, pp. 22–25, 41.
8. Simmons, G., Gumpert, J., & Rothman, B. Natural parents as partner in child case placement. *Social Casework*, April 1973, *54*, pp. 224–232.
9. Lee, J. A., & Swenson, C. R. Theory in action: A community social service agency. *Social Casework*, June 1978, *59*, p. 361.
10. Parkinson, ibid.

CHAPTER 14

1. Bryce, M. Home-based care: Development and rationale. In S. Maybanks & Bryce (Eds.), *Home-based services for children and families: Policy, practice, and research.* Springfield, Il: Charles C. Thomas, 1979, pp. 13–26.
2. Dunu, M. The Lower East Side family union: Assuring community services for minority families. In Maybanks & Bryce (Eds.), *Home-based services for children and families*, pp. 211–224.
3. Goldstein, H. Providing services to children in their own homes: An approach that can reduce foster placement. *Children Today*, July–August 1973, *2*, pp. 2–7.
4. Hirsch, J. S., Gailey, J., & Schmerl, E. A child welfare agency's program of

service to children in their own homes. *Child Welfare*, March 1976, *55*, pp. 193–204.

5. Jones, M. A. Reducing foster care through services to families. *Children Today*, November–December 1976, *5*, pp. 6–10.

6. National Clearinghouse for Home-Based Services to Children and Their Families. Home-based family centered service: A view from the child welfare sector. Oakdale: University of Iowa, 1978 (mimeographed).

7. Overton, A., Tinker, K., & associates. *Family Centered Project* (St. Paul, MN: Community Chest & Councils, 1957).

8. Ryan, M. Families program design: Giving families relevance in treatment: Maybanks & Bryce (Eds.) *Home-based services for children and families*, pp. 272–282.

9. Stephans, D. In-home family support services: An ecological systems approach. In Maybanks & Bryce (Eds.), *Home-based services for children and families*, pp. 283–295.

10. Tuszynski, A. & Dowd, J. An alternative approach to the treatment of protective service families. News and Views, *Social Casework*, March 1978 *59*, pp. 175–179.

11. National Clearinghouse for Home-Based Services to Children and Their Families, Cost effectiveness of home-based family centered service programs. Oakdale: University of Iowa, 1978 (mimeographed).

INDEX

Entries in italic type refer to core concepts of the book.

ABOUT THE AUTHOR

John Victor Compher, M.S.S., has for the past four years been a field instructor for numerous social work students, a supervisor for senior social work staff, and a community educator and in-service trainer for more than 100 professional audiences, locally, regionally, and nationally, in the area of family-based, child protective services. Prior to these experiences, he was a line social worker and a family therapist in public and private social service agencies in Philadelphia. In the early 1970s he helped to found a successful, alternative school for teenagers. Mr. Compher holds a masters degree in social services from The Bryn Mawr School of Social Work and Social Research and a bachelor of arts degree from King College. From his background in both psychodynamic and systems work, he has developed a practice that is both clinically based and systems-oriented. His articles have appeared in *Social Casework*, *Social Work*, and *Child Welfare* journals.